Mrs. Mary Woodyork
Box 123 - Hockessin, Del.
Phone 1548 -

Teachers College Studies in Education

LUCILE LINDBERG, Ed.D.

The
Democratic Classroom

A GUIDE FOR TEACHERS

BUREAU OF PUBLICATIONS

TEACHERS COLLEGE   COLUMBIA UNIVERSITY   NEW YORK

1954

Library of Congress Catalog Card Number 54-7854

Acknowledgments

It would be impossible to give credit to all the people whose ideas and experiences contributed to this study. Teachers in many parts of the country have permitted me to visit their classrooms and have helped to analyze the processes they were using. The pupils in the elementary schools where I taught for many years helped me formulate the basic ideas. Their frank criticisms of our ways of working together and their eagerness to refine those ways kept me continually searching with them for the means through which we could improve our classroom living.

It was Professor L. Thomas Hopkins who first gave me help in analyzing my role as a teacher. In recent years he has encouraged me to continue this analysis and to clarify it. He suggested that I organize this material so that it would be available for teachers who wish to work democratically with children.

Professor Goodwin Watson helped extend my vision of the role of the teacher in helping children become active participants in projects designed to improve their local, national, and world communities. Professor Alice Miel made helpful suggestions on planning, and Professor Jean Betzner contributed much to my ideas for developing a learning environment.

Many other professors at Teachers College have inspired and encouraged me to write this report. Several teachers in the field have read it and given constructive suggestions. I should like to express my appreciation for the help of everyone who made this book possible.

L. L.

Introduction

The tensions which continue to develop between nations and the misunderstandings that arise in our own country between groups and individuals are evidence that many people have not yet learned to live together effectively. Those who believe in a democratic way of life are convinced that harmonious relationships can be established and that people can meet the challenges of our complex, rapidly changing civilization if they understand democratic principles and put them into practice. Much of the responsibility for developing effective citizens must be assumed by the schools. Hence, emphasis is being placed to a greater extent than ever before on the teaching of democracy.

Many schools are giving children a wider variety of experiences and a more permissive classroom atmosphere. Teachers, through their studies of individual children and groups of children, are seeking ways to develop creative thinking and social skills. In many instances they make use of such techniques as role playing, socio-drama, and other types of sociometric devices. There is no doubt that this experimentation is resulting in some improvement of programs.

But democratic process must be a basic part of school programs if the teaching of democracy is to be effective. At present a great deal of effort seems to be directed toward perpetuating outworn patterns; there is little evidence of attempts to help children find ways of meeting new and emerging problem situations. Teachers need to study group process and to experiment with ways of using it. In order to meet needs intelligently both the experiences of the past and the resources of the present must be utilized intensively and extensively.

Emphasis on the teaching of democracy has been expressed in many books and articles published during the past ten years. Much has been written on subjects such as group dynamics, human relations, evaluation, and social attitudes. Specific help has been presented for improving group discussion, for developing projects, and for studying the interests of children. Such literature has undoubtedly had a part in improving practices. Too often, however, readers have considered the techniques or methods outlined as separate from the framework within which the author intended them to be used. When the suggestions have been applied under conditions for which they have not been designed, they have not accomplished their purposes.

This book is written for teachers who are already concerned about developing more democratic procedures and who have already done some experimentation. It is offered as a frame of reference within which they can examine their own ways of working. It is not expected that simply by reading it teachers will understand all the ways in which democracy can function in the classroom. Nor does this presentation provide specific directions for handling every situation that may arise.

Its purpose is to suggest ways of working through which children may acquire the skills they need for democratic living. It is easier to experiment in a school environment that encourages flexibility, but the examples cited show that even in very rigid situations it is possible to make changes. The examples have been selected from experiences which the author herself has had as a classroom teacher or has collected during visits to hundreds of classrooms. In many cases these classrooms were located in schools where experimentation was not encouraged.

Contents

The
Democratic Classroom

CHAPTER I

Group Process and Education

The philosophy underlying democracy is being questioned. In many parts of the world, it is assumed that the so-called common man will follow the dictates of those in authority. To people who accept such an assumption, the concept that every individual can and should participate in making decisions that affect him seems unsound. They fear that widespread participation in making decisions will slow down progress. Even in our own country there are shortcomings that must be remedied if democracy is to continue. When faced with a crisis, some people resort to authoritarian techniques for the sake of expediency because they feel that democratic ways of working are cumbersome and slow. They do not believe that their common problems can be solved effectively through cooperative effort.

Those who use democratic process are aware of its strength. Inasmuch as doubts are being raised concerning its effectiveness, those who believe in it must re-examine their manner of living to see whether or not the procedures being practiced are truly democratic.

It is important that children acquire deep convictions of the value of democracy. These convictions, however, do not have much value unless implemented by knowledge of how to live democratically. So long as children attain insight into the philosophy underlying democracy and learn the skills needed to put it into practice, the democratic way of life may be expected to survive; but in our complex culture, they may not be able to gain

1

the perspective needed to see how it functions without guidance. It is important, therefore, to make certain that school programs are providing this help.

Process—The Essence of Democracy

The essence of democracy is group process. Democratic group process is a means through which people locate, define, and study their own needs and continuously improve their methods of meeting these needs. Through working together, no matter how intense the needs that are felt, no matter how complex the problems to be met, no matter how important the decisions to be made, this process can be used effectively. When reference is made in this book to group process or to democratic process, or simply to process, it is the democratic group process, as defined above, which is intended.

Many people accept the privileges of a democratic way of life without knowing that its very existence depends upon group process. Instead of using group process to make intelligent decisions themselves, they unthinkingly use patterns of behavior that have been worked out by others. If the situations they face remain relatively static, they are able to live in a way that seems satisfactory to them; but when new sets of circumstances or problems arise, they grasp at any suggestions that are offered.

To try to meet the needs of one situation by applying patterns that have proved successful in other situations is a static approach to life. Even though the patterns have been developed through group process, when they are isolated from that process they become static. The quality of living in a democracy depends upon the quality of the process used in making decisions.

ELEMENTS OF PROCESS

Any attempt to identify the elements of democratic process is likely to be misleading. Readers may interpret suggestions as a pattern for action even though the fact that there can be no set plan of procedure is carefully explained in advance. In spite of the limitations involved, an attempt will be made to identify the elements of this process so that teachers may help children to use them. While democratic procedures are never exactly the same in any two situations, an examination of the way the process

2

operates brings to light certain common elements. If the process is to retain its dynamic quality, each of these elements must be included:

Identification of need by members of the group

Cooperative formulation of plans through which to satisfy the identified need

Involvement in action suggested by the plans

Continual evaluation of planning and action

Increased understanding of the significance of the process

Although five elements of the democratic process have been identified, they should not be considered as distinct, step-by-step procedures. Rather, they are inter-functioning elements which are embedded in the total process. One phase of the process leads to the next and overlaps it. Planning is begun and possible resources are considered even while needs are being identified, so that before final decisions are made it is possible to know whether it will be satisfying to do the work under consideration. Evaluation goes on during the entire process.

A PRIMARY CONCERN IN THE SCHOOL PROGRAM

The responsibility of the school for teaching children the skills necessary for effective living in a democracy has already been pointed out. That the quality of living achieved in a democracy depends upon the insights of its citizens into the nature and functioning of the group process has also been called to the attention of the reader. It is therefore apparent that helping children learn to use the democratic process should be the school's first concern. Group process must be thoroughly understood if children are to use it with confidence to meet their needs.

If group process is to be a primary concern in school programs, then the extent to which children are learning to practice it in actual classroom situations must be a basic criterion for evaluating school programs. Undoubtedly, it is easier to implement group process in a situation where the physical arrangements can be adapted to the needs of the group and where administrators allow teachers freedom to experiment. There are, however, some teachers who are helping children to work together in spite of rigid working conditions.

The manner in which teachers work with children is highly important. If children spend day after day trying to find the answers which someone else has decided ahead of time are right, they learn to depend upon some person "above them" instead of upon themselves or the group. It is difficult for children to learn that a democratic approach is practical when the problems which develop during their own classroom living are being met by an autocratic course of action. After they have become adjusted to the pseudo-efficiency of such practices, the slow manner in which democracy operates is likely to be discouraging. Instead of working enthusiastically to put into practice the philosophy they have learned to voice, the children are likely to take one of two paths. They may always do as someone else tells them, or they may rebel and refuse to seek advice from anyone. In both cases, the basic principles of democracy are denied.

Ways Democracy Is Being Taught in the Schools

A study of the ways democracy is now being taught in the schools shows that in most schools emphasis is not being placed upon a practical use of process. Some teachers are trying to give children practice in democratic living, but there are many misconceptions of how to do it. Some teachers feel that their classrooms are democratic if they have movable furniture, an abundance of art supplies, attractively decorated rooms, evidences of activity, and committee work in progress.

Some teachers think that children are learning to be democratic if they are free to express themselves in any manner they desire and if no standards to be attained are in evidence. These same teachers often take it for granted that colleagues whose classrooms seem to show little activiy, or who work in a closely organized way, are not trying to be democratic. By the same token, some teachers feel that they are working democratically with children if they are making the work interesting.

A look at some of the ways democracy is being taught may give perspective to a consideration of the kind of program needed. Each approach will be considered from the point of view of the concept of democracy implied in it, its assumptions concerning the way children learn, and the extent to which they learn democratic skills.

Children are taught behavior patterns and rules for conduct. Underlying this approach is the concept that democracy is based on behavior patterns, which one generation passes on to the next. These patterns are supposed to dictate the kind of action that will be acceptable in a particular type of situation.

There are two quite different viewpoints concerning the ways children should be taught these patterns. The first takes for granted that children who have studied rules for conduct will be able to put them into action without further help. Rigid observance of rules will have varying effects. Some children will learn to accept authority and be helpless to act unless directed. Others may learn to resent authority so much that when freed from close supervision they defy any kind of guidance and become quite undisciplined. The manners they have been taught are thrown aside when there is no one to enforce their use.

The other viewpoint is that children must learn behavior patterns through practice. Perhaps, for example, they are expected to learn consideration for others and cooperation by acting out assigned roles at a make-believe party, but children are not likely to identify such artificial experiences with those they meet in real life.

Such methods are not likely to teach children to make a dynamic attack on new problems. Rather, they assume that the transfer of learning from one situation to another is automatic. Observation of pupil behavior, however, prevents our believing that merely learning rules of conduct or practicing behavior patterns in hypothetical situations will ensure their being understood, valued, or followed.

Children are taught the political structure of our democracy. The concept here is that democracy is primarily political. It is assumed that democracy rises or falls according to the extent to which its basic political structure remains intact and that forms of government different from ours must be less democratic. Therefore, when educating children in democracy, knowledge of the mechanics of government is considered most important. Thus the schools proceed on the theory that children will know how to work effectively in their society when they have received information about the government. For example, they are asked to memorize the Preamble to the Constitution and the Bill of Rights. What the school seems to be ignoring is the fact that a successful society is based on good human relationships. That an individual has an intellectual understanding of politics is no guarantee that

5

he will be a useful, effective citizen. It must be remembered that government is only the vehicle for the operation of the democratic process.

Children are taught the symbols of democracy. Much importance is attached to developing group unity through patriotic observances such as reciting creeds, singing, and participating in frequent ceremonials. Such symbols are felt to be a means of obtaining enthusiastic support. It is assumed that continuous observance of appropriate ceremonies will maintain the attitudes required of democratic citizens and that each individual will learn democracy through its symbols. Therefore, in the school program the teaching of symbols is given a significant place.

Intellectual understanding is so completely ignored and such great reliance is placed on emotional appeal that chiefly the superficial aspects of democracy are dealt with. Through participation in patriotic ceremonies, children undoubtedly receive emotional satisfaction. It cannot be taken for granted, however, that emotionalizing the appropriate symbols and rituals prepares them to make decisions that will improve the quality of their living.

Children are taught the democratic tradition in the history of our nation. Those who take this approach conceive of democracy as a historical tradition only. They feel that to retain that tradition, children must review the events through which democracy has evolved, and that they will recognize the worth of democracy when they see it in proper historical perspective. It is assumed that children will develop the insight needed to work democratically today if they have a thorough knowledge of the struggles that brought democracy into being and of the perpetual vigilance their forefathers had to maintain in order to survive pressures exerted by other traditions. A study of the achievements of their forefathers is thought to give children sufficient basis for becoming very democratic. So widespread is this point of view that the legislators of many states have passed laws requiring schools to include American history courses in their curriculums.

In evaluating this approach as a means of helping children develop democratic skills and ideals, concern must be expressed that so much is taught about the history of democracy and that so little attention is given to its implications for the world of today. This approach, like the others, assumes that when children learn a particular body of knowledge, related skills develop automatically. It loses much of its supposed value when this assumption is questioned.

Children participate in student councils and student courts. Democracy is considered chiefly a means for making rules and settling disputes; since democracy can be learned best through practice, setting up councils and courts in school will give children the experience they need.

In some situations what is done is so carefully planned and so closely supervised by the principal that the children's ideas are seldom called for. In other situations children are left relatively unsupervised. They make as many rules as they wish, but the adults accept only those that they consider sensible. Usually the children do not improve their ways of working, and the attitudes they develop are often damaging. In the one instance they are likely to see democracy as synonymous with dictatorship; in the other, they have no conception of discipline. Their verdicts are often unsympathetic, and they mete out punishments that good teachers would never use.

Children are taught techniques of democracy in isolation from the process. In many classrooms the democratic process is considered simply a set of procedures rather than an on-going way of working together. Techniques are taught but opportunity is not provided for using them in meaningful situations. There may be daily teacher-pupil planning periods but they are held so that the children will learn these techniques, not because they are needed for effective group operation. Thus democratic procedures become just an additional subject in the curriculum.

It is expected, however, that techniques learned in isolation can be put into practice when appropriate circumstances arise. But children see these procedures merely as time-consuming devices and do not attach any special significance to them; for they know that the plans will not be satisfactory unless they coincide with those made previously by the teacher. To them the planning periods are guessing games, the object of which is to find out what the teacher wishes them to do.

These approaches are used with varying degrees of skill. Each of them may be used in an interesting or in a boring way. No matter how they are taught, none of them will in and of itself

7

give children adequate experience in democratic living. Some of them may be helpful, however, if they are included as part of a program.

The Teacher—A Specialist in Process

Knowledge and understanding of group process is the important contribution a teacher has to make to any group of children. He must bring it to the children's attention through the way he works. He sets it in motion and guides its movement. Learning the skills involved in defining needs, planning and working together to meet them, and using the results of thoughtful evaluation require much careful practice and study. Children cannot be expected to learn them merely through hearing them explained.

The teacher's responsibility is to help children to examine their problems and use group process to seek solutions for them. Children can be taught to recognize the importance of all the elements in the process and become increasingly expert in making use of them. The teacher's time will not be completely absorbed with the techniques of group procedures. As a specialist in democratic process, he will serve in many capacities. He needs to know and understand the characteristics of children. He should have a broad background of practical knowledge and be desirous of increasing his experience. To work democratically requires delving into many matters on both the child and the adult level. The teacher should be so familiar with the real problems of the local community that he is able to help children find ways of studying and working on those which are of most direct concern to them. He needs to understand social issues at local, national, and international levels so that he can help children see themselves in an ever-widening setting. Unless the teacher has great depth of understanding and breadth of knowledge the children's vision may be limited.

The chapters that follow will show how the teacher uses his background of experience in helping children to develop skill in the elements of the democratic group process. Although these elements are interactive, the role of the teacher in relation to each of them will be examined separately.

CHAPTER II

Identifying and Defining Needs

Every person is constantly attempting to maintain his equilibrium in the face of forces, both external and internal, which tend to disturb him. When a disturbance is felt so strongly that an individual, unable to tolerate it any longer, changes his behavior in order to dispel it, we shall, in this book, say that he is attempting to meet a need.

There are many ways of meeting a need. All will not, however, result in equal satisfaction. The degree of satisfaction achieved will be directly related to the quality of the process used in meeting it. The ways in which people attempt to satisfy needs are learned. Over a period of time, an individual finds that some approaches seem to result in greater satisfaction than do others. Hence, he calls on these more and more frequently. Sometimes people proceed in a hit-or-miss fashion and do not know in the end what really did contribute to the satisfaction.

Since the needs people feel are the motivating forces underlying behavior, it is important that people learn to satisfy them in the most effective way. When children come to school, they have already developed some ways of meeting needs. These patterns can be modified. Helping children to modify the processes they have already learned and to develop new ones is a basic objective in a democratic classroom.

Many teachers study the home backgrounds of children, help them adjust to group living, provide materials adapted to their abilities, and develop their hobbies and interests, because they wish to help children meet the needs they are feeling in their daily living. These concerns are particularly apparent in programs where special attention is given to providing for individual differences; they are apparent even in classrooms where all the children are required to complete the same rigid assignments, where harsh consequences sometimes result when such requirements are not met. There, teachers use pages of arithmetic problems, lists of spelling words, and series of exercises in capitalization and punctuation to make certain that every child acquires certain skills which they consider to be basic needs.

Although the primary purpose of these two approaches is meeting needs, there is a wide difference of opinion on what the needs are and on the types of procedures to be used in filling them. In schools where faculty groups have worked together to improve the curriculum, the same questions are raised again and again. One question area is, Whose needs shall be satisfied? Shall the curriculum be geared to the needs of society or to those of each individual child? Do the needs of society and those of individual children differ?

Another vital question area is, Who shall select the problems on which the programs will be based? Shall such decisions be made by the state, by local authorities, by teachers, by children? Shall a highly organized course of study be prepared? Shall teachers depend upon textbook writers to set forth the kinds of knowledge children shall study? Or shall the findings of experts in child development and curriculum construction determine what shall be studied? Can a teacher determine the most important needs? Do children know what their needs are?

Additional questions are, What needs shall be met? Shall an effort be made to determine the kind of life children will live as adults and to develop the school program to prepare them for that life? Or shall the curriculum be based on their present-day needs with efforts directed toward enabling them to work well on the problems which they are facing now?

These questions are answered in many ways. Sometimes teachers decide upon courses of action in such controversial areas without considering carefully the implications involved. Their answers should be in keeping with their general philosophy and with a sound concept of learning. In a country ruled by a dictator, teachers expect the content of the curriculum to be determined by someone who represents the state. Since the people are expected to remain subservient to the state, the school program is so planned that the chief effort goes toward training children in the skills they must use to serve the state. Those in command attempt to visualize what the state will be and the kind of people it will require, and to describe the model persons the school should turn out. Lists of needs are outlined by experts or by those who are set up as experts. This mode of operation is consistent with the kind of philosophy that permeates all life in such cultures.

In a democracy, on the other hand, final authority rests with the people. Government exists so that each individual may, through his cooperation with others, develop a more satisfying life. The people decide what kind of life they would like to have and which problems shall receive the greatest part of their attention. Plans to attain a better life for the future revolve around working to improve the present.

Basic issues concerning curriculum selection should be examined in light of this democratic philosophy. In view of the importance of the individual, teachers should direct their attention toward helping children to meet their own needs. They should prepare them to organize their living in the way that will best serve them, rather than prepare children to fit into one particular kind of organization.

It follows also that children should play an important part in deciding which needs they will try to meet and in defining the problems upon which they will work. They should make their selection cooperatively. They do not live alone in the world, so when decisions are made everyone must be considered.

Everything that children learn may serve as preparation for adult life, but the problems studied should be related to their immediate, present-day living. These problems will vary from group to group and from generation to generation. A set of needs to be met or a required list of problems to be solved cannot be outlined in advance.

One task of the teacher is to guide children in learning intelligent ways of identifying needs. This is a basic part of the process to be learned, even though problems differ from group to group and the actual knowledge gained in working on them

11

will vary. As their control of the process increases, their power to improve living will increase also.

Psychologically, this approach to identifying needs works to the best interest of all because what is being learned is related to the need felt by the individual. When children are taught skills and knowledge in which they feel no interest and for which they see no use, so-called learnings are easily forgotten and teachers find themselves engaged in a frustrating cycle of teaching and re-teaching. When children are solving problems important to them, which will make a difference in their own living, learning becomes a part of their experience and they can make use of this knowledge in other situations. The result of a child's effort to meet needs that are real to him far surpass results attained by his working on problems that have significance for others but not for him.

Many teachers hold the mistaken idea that if children are to cooperate in the selection of problems, the teacher is only required to gather the children together and ask enthusiastically some such question as, Children, what do you want to study? A group of children confronted with a question like this may respond in at least two ways. They may think the question very silly or they may not comprehend what is wanted. In either case, the teacher may meet dead silence. Urging might bring forth some suggestions. The kinds of things the children might mention would depend very largely on the relationships that had existed previously between them and the teacher and on the kinds of activities which they have learned to expect to carry on. They may respond dutifully with a long list of grammatical skills which they think are what the teacher wants them to learn. They may suggest fantastic ideas which really have little or no interest for them, but which place the spotlight on the children who make the suggestions. In any case, the teacher cannot expect such a procedure to succeed. Yet many teachers have tried this approach or one equally unplanned. Not achieving desirable results, they then become convinced that children cannot play a significant part in the selection process.

Children do not arrive in the classroom with their needs already neatly defined. At least until they have had considerable experience in working together, they may not be able to express these needs verbally. They respond to questions about them impulsively without the consideration that comes from experience. The teacher plays a very important part in helping children to identify their needs and to become cognizant of how they are currently attempting to meet them. He helps them to develop increasingly more satisfying ways of resolving them.

Needs are met through the experiences children have. The teacher helps children select the kinds of exprience by which they can work through their needs together in the classroom. These experiences are derived from the areas of interest of the children. Some of these interests are of long duration, others have been newly acquired.

Selecting Interests

The areas of interest from which a group of children makes its selection may develop in many ways. Sometimes they develop spontaneously because of the obvious lacks in the children's own environment. For example, when children do not have the materials they require, they may make definite plans for securing them. Such plans may involve many kinds of action over a long period of time.

Often deep interests are discovered as children and teacher talk together, sharing ideas and activities in which they as individuals are engaged. When Ray brought his telegraph set into one fifth grade, a whole new area of interest arose. Almost all the children wanted to make their own sets. Those who did not build sets often borrowed from others. An intricate communication system was set up with an eighth grade science class in another part of the building.

Sometimes interests develop because of some unusual happening in the community. A hurricane was the beginning point for one fourth grade group. A bad accident was the impetus for another. Both these incidents called to the children's attention areas of study with which they had not been concerned before. Sometimes a teacher points out problems. His knowledge of the group may lead him to believe that they may find these problems of vital concern. Sometimes teacher and children sit down together to see what kind of work might develop if they were to investigate any of these problems.

Whatever the seeming concern, regardless of its origin, a

teacher cannot know how deeply an interest is felt, he cannot know how important it is to children, until the group has had an opportunity to explore it together. While an area may have been discovered through a spontaneous display of enthusiasm, the areas to which children give large portions of their time in this kind of program must be selected by the group very deliberately. A group cannot give its complete attention to every interest that is felt. Some are dealt with quickly as they arise and some are put aside for future study. The teachers realize that these may contain the seeds for later work the group will do.

The teacher's most important work is done in connection with those interests which the group deliberately chooses. The selection of experiences by the children themselves is a part of the process. The dynamic quality of group process is in the interaction which results when a group examines its own needs and determines which are most pressing. If children are to see this process in true perspective, they must work together on some problems that are of long enough duration so that every element of the process comes clearly into focus. Otherwise, children are not likely to grasp the full significance of its movement.

Although the teacher does not select the areas of interest to be pursued, he must provide some definite contributions toward guiding the children to select wisely. In the sections that follow, the role of the teacher in this guidance will be discussed.

Enriching the Classroom Environment

The teacher works toward enriching the classroom environment as a means of helping the children to deepen already existing interests and to develop new interests through a creative use of school facilities. Experiences provided by the school, however, are not limited to things to be read, looked at, or played with. Excursions, films, and community resources are important also. The experiences offered should include many which focus children's attention on underlying values or help them recognize basic economic and social problems concerned with democratic progress.

From the very beginning, the teacher should make it clear that he and the children are jointly responsible for providing experiences. A teacher working alone cannot possibly provide the variety which children and teacher working together can provide. Enriched living results when cooperative efforts lead to continuous exploration.

MATERIAL RESOURCES

The use of material resources encourages ideas which lead to more ideas. From these resources children broaden their interests into realms far beyond those where the materials themselves might be expected to lead. The teacher should introduce materials of many descriptions. His own contributions to the classroom inspire the children to participate in adding things of interest.

Among the most stimulating things a teacher can introduce are books and other reading materials. They should include all the areas in which the teacher has noted interest as well as those in which a new interest might develop. There should be a wide range of reading levels. An attractive nook where children can browse makes reading inviting.

Bulletin boards can display pictures, which will encourage children to bring additional pictures and materials for exhibit. A file of pictures and pamphlets will stimulate children's interest and will grow as the children add their own informational resources.

Materials salvaged from neighborhood scrap heaps or provided by either teachers or children can lead to other interests. A few such items might be magnets, batteries, the motor of a car, a radio, a typewriter, or an adding machine. With such a beginning the children will be encouraged to add a motley array of other items.

Every classroom should have some materials with which children may try new roles and act out their problems. Often they will express through this action hopes and fears they would not verbalize. Such materials are not hard to accumulate. Any classroom can have a costume box containing plumed hats, neckties, vests, an evening dress, a pocketbook, a pair of high-heeled slippers.

Furniture and equipment used by such specialized groups as doctors, dentists, nurses, plumbers, or masons provide many opportunities for exploration and the exercise of active imagination. In one school, the top of an old kitchen cabinet contained such ingredients as cinnamon, sugar, salt, flour. The children frequently mixed dough or made frosting for their graham crackers. The addition of a stethoscope to the box of play equipment brought a quick change in the cabinet's function. It became the medicine room for a hospital, which was established by using tables as beds.

Not all the materials that might provoke interest and broaden outlook in a classroom can be listed. One group may be fascinated by objects that another group will cast aside with a glance. A rooster's head would certainly not be included in a list yet when one was proudly deposited on a teacher's desk it became the starting point of profitable discussion.

Merely collecting materials does not ensure broadening interests. Many teachers have accumulated materials in their classrooms without really enriching the children's living. These classrooms appear to be stimulating places in which children can grow. The shelves are filled with interesting reading materials attractively displayed. Bulletin boards with gay borders and well-cut captions display pictures. Science tables hold carefully labeled specimens. A well-stocked aquarium contains beautiful fish. Magnets and sets of batteries are available for experiments. But the children examine the materials in a halfhearted, desultory manner, if at all. The rooms belong to the teachers, who have arranged them, and the children are likely to leave them for the teachers to enjoy. Undemocratic practices can exist in an attractive, well supplied classroom, as well as in one which is starved for materials.

The keynote, then, to using materials as a means for extending interests is in the children's participation, rather than in the accumulation of numerous items. When the teacher accepts and appreciates the first offerings the children bring in, he is encouraging them to add anything else they value. At first the children will not distinguish between the kinds of contributions they make, but they will become selective as they learn what things seem useful and what things seem merely to take up space. As they find creative ways of using what they do bring, they become increasingly aware of the materials about them.

The accumulation of materials may stimulate a need for group cooperation. As equipment and supplies are brought into the classroom, arrangements must be made for a place to put them. The teacher may ask such questions as: Where can we put these things? What kind of working space is needed if we are to get the most value from them?

The children of one group were spending a great deal of time searching for the books they wanted. Instead of rearranging the books himself, the teacher called the problem to the attention of the children. Did they find the present arrangement inconvenient? What could be done about it? As a result of the discussion aroused, the children investigated to find such information as the following: How were the books in the school library arranged? In the neighborhood library? Were there other, more helpful ways of arranging them? Would the library lend them a bookshelf? Were there empty bookshelves in a vacant classroom? Could they get materials from the lumberyard? Could they requisition supplies from the central office? Would apple boxes or orange crates be usable as shelves?

In another school, fifth graders were asked by one of the parents if they could use an old divan. The children decided they wanted it for their reading corner but they had to solve many problems before they could accept it. How would they bring it to the school? Would the adult class in upholstery repair it for for them? How could they be sure it was free from infectious germs?

As children work together to improve living arrangements in their own classrooms they discover still more materials and develop many new interests. In rearranging their books, the first group described found it necessary to get boxes, to order paint, and to equip a work bench. The work bench became the center of many other activities; the orange crates were used in building scenery for a play. The group which received the divan had to locate and use fumigating and antiseptic materials. Their interest in such materials led them to establish a system for disinfecting their feet after taking showers.

HUMAN RESOURCES

Children are likely to come to school with the idea that their only resources are materials such as books and art supplies. The teacher must help them to discover the importance of human resources. Children often fail to consider the people in the community as sources of information and help. Through interaction with the community a high level of social development is gained.

As with material resources, the teacher initiates this interest through the example he himself sets. Through his participation, the children are able to see the role of other adults as resource people. When the teacher is unable to help in some area, he suggests that they find someone else who has specialized in that area and can give the needed direction.

When children are grappling with a problem that seems to demand greater experience than they have had, when they lack skill, when they fail to see all sides of an issue, the teacher may ask them to consider means for getting help. The question, Who could help with this? often starts children on a search for the suitable person. The teacher may call their attention to the specialized abilities of other adults in the building. Principal, custodian, dietician, and other teachers have much to offer. The examples below illustrate how children can be helped to see the need for and to search for the people who can help them meet their needs.

In one classroom the teacher asked the children if they had noticed that the nail supply was getting low. What would they do when the nails were gone? A trip to the principal's office made it clear that there were no more. A survey of their homes showed that they could not get help from that source. The custodian did not have nails to give them, but he offered help. He showed them how they could get the same strength with half as many nails by spacing them. They wondered how he knew so much about it and were surprised to learn that he had done carpentry work for many years.

Resource people not only help children when they must acquire skills or information but also help in extending children's interests. One teacher often has an artist friend spend the afternoon in the classroom painting with water colors. The children go over and watch as he works at the easel. Many of them paint busily themselves. Respect for creative effort is developed as well as interest in water color.

When firemen inspected the building during Fire Prevention Week, one teacher asked them to show the children what was in the fire extinguisher which hung in the hall outside their door. The firemen let all the children have a close look, then they went outside for a practical demonstration. In the weeks that followed, the children demonstrated the operation of many kinds of extinguishers. They visited the firehouse so that they could see how lifesaving equipment is used.

In another school, a teacher who was visiting a pupil's home admired the attractive flower arrangements. She later suggested to the other children of the class that Alfred's mother might show them how to make such flower arrangements for their classroom. The children made careful plans for securing many flowers before they issued an invitation to Mrs. Anderson. Later in the year when they wanted to do something special for their mothers, they remembered what Mrs. Anderson had said about winter corsages and sent a committee over to get some suggestions from her. The children learned a great deal about the arrangement of flowers. A neighbor who had assumed little or no significance in their thinking became an interesting person to them. They saw value, also, in talents which they had previously considered unimportant.

Visitors from other countries are also valuable resource people. Problems of the local community are seen in better perspective as children look with others at similar problems which exist in another culture. Care should be taken that many cultural aspects of the country, the home problems, and the relationships of people are emphasized, rather than the bizarre and spectacular.

Children serve as resources for each other. Every child has something special to offer. It is easy to recognize this when the child's home culture differs markedly from that of the other children, but those with a different cultural background are not the only ones who enrich living in the classroom. Every child can do this. It takes time to find out just what children's special abilities are. Sometimes during the course of the year a child develops special abilities or gains special knowledge.

A teacher looking back over a semester with a group of children listed some ways in which children had served as resources. A part of the list follows:

John played the accordion.
Raymond showed how the notes are formed on the trombone.
Sue showed others how to make puppet clothes.
Marcia played the piano for the assembly program.
Charlie organized the group for quick action when plaster fell down from the ceiling.
Harold gave firsthand information on skunks.

Judy brought a collection of sea shells.
Susan brought several records.
Joe brought sample ballots for the whole class.
Ramona brought printed materials on prejudice.

An accident or unusual circumstance may enlarge interest and encourage activity. When Harry was stricken with infantile paralysis his family was given the funds necessary to give him adequate hospital care. Since it was money raised in the March of Dimes drive that made these funds available for Harry, his classmates developed an interest in the drive. They decided to try to raise money by giving a carnival in the gym. The children from other rooms came to try the games of skill which had been devised. After expenses had been subtracted, a total of six dollars and forty-seven cents was given to the March of Dimes. The next year they decided that instead of having a carnival they would solicit the help of children in other classes by publicizing and explaining the purposes for which the money was used.

When the children in a group fail to recognize the possibility of many attitudes concerning a problem, interviewing those who hold opposing ideas may broaden their horizons. Tiny children constantly attempt to explore new equipment and new relationships. If permitted they will go into every drawer and cupboard in their homes. They test the behavior of all adults whom they meet. This desire to expand interests should be encouraged. Given opportunities, children will include more and more people in their thinking while they plan to improve their own living.

Children in one school interviewed the principal, PTA officials, members of the City Council, and the Mayor in their attempt to find out why the funds for a new school building which had been promised were suddenly removed from the budget. When they failed to receive satisfactory answers they interviewed members of the League of Women Voters to find out where they could get additional information. Every father and mother became a resource person and a working companion as the children sought to find out on what basis people had decided to vote for these officials.

In another school real estate agents and home owners were consulted as children attempted to find out why Jews were discouraged from buying property in certain areas. Since this practice was affecting members of their own group, they surveyed other areas of the city to see whether or not discrimination existed elsewhere. When the children found that it did, they interviewed members of local groups that are fighting discrimination to see what they could do to help.

Encouraging Exploration

Children should be encouraged to investigate their environment. Many teachers push very hard to have them select an area for study because they feel that time is being wasted unless the children are launched on some common group activity at once. They fail to realize that children learn a great deal as they explore.

In developing a stimulating environment, the teacher's most important function is to create an atmosphere where the children feel free to explore. No matter how many experiences are available, in order to obtain maximum value from them, children must enjoy them. The formalized tea parties, telephone conversations, and puppet shows provided by some teachers offer practically no opportunity for creativity or experimentation. If the teacher is to be helped in locating needs by a study of the behavior of children, he must help the children to feel free to behave naturally and spontaneously.

The teacher's personality is the most important influence in determining the kind of spirit there will be. A teacher with an inflexible personality can make movable furniture seem immovable, while a creative teacher can work cooperatively with a group of children to overcome the limitations of immovable furniture. The materials in a situation will be helpful only if children have an opportunity to explore and use them. In the illustrations that follow, the materials were the same but the human relationships were different, and the difference was one that all the material things in the world could not have changed.

In one classroom, furniture had been unscrewed, supplies were abundant, and almost ideal physical arrangements had been made. But the teacher so controlled the situation that the children waited mute and expressionless as she wet and spread out paper and measured out the exact amount of paint that would be needed. The children were not given an opportunity to experiment with materials.

With similar facilities, the teacher in another room was able to provide a classroom climate that encouraged creativity. The children were delighted when she supplied a recipe for finger paint and helped them cook it as it was needed. They were thrilled to put in color and make it pink, then red, and then dark red. A bucket of water was nearby so that when they wished to finger paint they could wet the paper and make as many paintings as they wanted. Sometimes they spilled or dripped both paint and water, but the teacher had sponges available so they could clean the floor. Freed from close supervision, they experimented with many kinds of designs, they tried many color combinations, and they dabbled just for the fun of dabbling.

Children will be able to explore in an open, forward-looking manner if they know that the experiences they have had and are having are valuable. In addition, they must realize that questions are a means for finding out many things, that they are not expected to know everything. Let us see how children can gain confidence in these two areas.

VALUE OF PERSONAL EXPERIENCES

Children often fail to see that accounts of their own experiences make worth-while group contributions. Exploring becomes much more meaningful when children find out what others are enjoying and show others what they themselves find interesting. Properly handled, periods of sharing provide opportunity for children to receive the necessary encouragement.

The teacher must assume responsibility for helping children get this needed encouragement. He begins on the first day of school through the respect he shows each contributor and each contribution during the discussion period. Most teachers try to make these beginning periods especially informal. Perhaps they ask what the children have done during the summer. Children who have traveled are most likely to volunteer first, and in their excitement many may speak at once.

In one classroom, John was quick to say that he had been to Florida. He had seen people diving and swimming, and he gave an impromptu demonstration of a discovery he made about diving—if you stand tall and stretch your arms high you do not go into the water as fast as if you hunch into a ball and let yourself fall in.

22

Ray had seen peanuts growing in Virginia. The other children had not known that peanuts grew. "Can children in Virginia go out and pick up peanuts whenever they wish?" No one quite knew the answer to that one but the teacher suggested some ways in which they might find out.

After such interesting happenings had been related by those who had taken trips, the ones who had stayed in town all summer could have felt that they had no contribution to make. But the teacher helped them see that local happenings are of interest too. Harry had seen one of the big league players. Hannah's aunt had come and brought her a doll with "Made in Czechoslovakia" written on it. Ramona had gone to dinner with one of her mother's friends in a hotel, where she had used a finger bowl.

If some children say they have not done anything interesting, the teacher draws them out. Even shy children contribute when someone shows genuine interest in what they have done. The group enjoys hearing about the good time some children had the day they climbed to the top of the garage. Games of prize-fight in the sandbox and cops and robbers in the back alley make exciting telling and wonderful listening when the teacher, with a few well stated questions, helps them play up the interesting parts.

There may be children in the group who are new to the neighborhood. When did they move here? Near whom do they live? What kind of school did they go to last year? The teacher helps each child gain new dignity through contributing. Even in the first informal meeting he discerns some interests that can be extended if they seem important enough to the children.

The initial interest which children and teacher show in each other's experiences should continue throughout the year. Classroom explorations will be shared and thus new interests will spread. Several people working on an interest will unearth possibilities in it which would not occur to one or two people exploring alone. The more worth-while the children feel their experiences have been the more eagerly they will undertake others. Thus, they learn to develop great power in exploring. They dig more and more deeply into areas that interest them. If they are given even a little encouragement, they will search diligently for ways of improving their environment.

FREEDOM TO ASK QUESTIONS

Children should feel free to ask for help. They should not be ashamed of asking question which may not have deep significance for anyone else.

The story is told of a boy who had run away from home. When he was found and asked why he had run away he said, "I wanted to learn something." Further queries brought out these explanations. "I can't learn at home because they keep asking me what I learned at school. I can't learn at school because we spend most of our time correcting our homework assignments and the teacher expects you to know how to get everything right."

If children are rebuffed or made to feel that they should already know, to ask for help does not seem to be a respectable thing to do. Since needs are often revealed through questions children ask, the learning climate must be one in which they feel free to ask.

An experience with a group of sixth grade boys illustrates what can happen when such freedom is felt. When they came into the classroom one afternoon, it was evident that something exciting was afoot. "We want to know how to figure baseball averages," they said, as they clustered around the teacher's desk. "The same thing isn't going to happen this spring that happened last year; when it is time to get a team together, we will know where we stand." They produced a sports page from a newspaper and showed her exactly what they meant. A few queries showed that some of them had a fairly good idea of the basis on which the averages were figured, but no one seemed to know the method by which they were figured. They listened eagerly to a short explanation of the reasons that averages come out the way they do. The teacher figured averages for three of the boys and soon all were at the board hard at work. She made several visits to the playground where averages were being figured, using chalk on the hard-surfaced playground, before all had the basic understandings and were working correctly. This phase of percentage became easy for the boys. They began to use percentage in other situations. The teacher did not take their request for help in figuring averages to mean that they wanted to study every phase of percentage. Baseball was the focal point, rather than percentages. This valuable experience was possible because the children's teacher had already shown that she was willing to help them meet their needs.

Children often ask questions concerning reasons for existing conditions in their communities. "Why are the streets in some parts of the city clean while ours are littered with garbage?" or "Why can't my dad get a job? Just because he's a Negro? That's no reason. Why is it?"

The children in one fourth grade were greatly disturbed because their community was infested by rats. One baby sister had even been bitten. The children aroused enough concern among local groups so that a drive was made to alleviate the immediate situation. During their investigation while they were doing research on how they could arouse the community, they were asking questions that took them into still broader fields. "How did such conditions arise in the first place? Why were such high rents charged for terrible apartments?"

The teacher recorded each question so the children could go as far in their search for answers as was possible for fourth graders. They left many questions unanswered but they had developed an attitude which ensured that those same questions and many additional ones would be asked again and again.

EXPANSION OF EXPLORATION

Children's investigations often take them outside the four walls of their own classroom. A teacher, however, can find a great deal to stimulate their questions and ideas right in their own building and immediate community even in a school where long excursions are not permitted.

In order to make the problems upon which the children work increasingly significant, the teacher tries to provide for and helps the children provide for themselves experiences which improve relationships and raise the quality of living in the whole building. At first a class may be selfish and possessive, but as relationships in the group improve they begin to feel the power of cooperative efforts and learn to include others.

The children of one fifth grade changed their area of need-satisfaction from one which included only themselves to one which included many others. They built an elaborate puppet theater. They were pleased to give performances for other classes but almost resented it when other classes invited them in to see a show. They often criticized the makeshift stages used. They wished to be the only group engaging in a puppet project. The teacher suggested they work out a loan arrangement so that other groups could use their stage. At first they resisted the idea and the teacher did not insist. As they worked with the children in other rooms on other school projects, such as assembly programs, newspaper, lunchroom arrangements, and improvement of playground activities, constructive relationships were built. The children saw the advantages that are gained from sharing. Before the year was over, they were offering their puppet stage to anyone who wished to use it.

Conditions in the whole building were improved by the fifth grade children in one suburban community. After several days of rainy weather which kept them inside during the noon hour, children were complaining bitterly about their hard luck. Some places, they said, had decent facilities for basketball, volley ball, and other sports, but their own playrooms, while large, had low ceilings. As the discussion proceeded, the teacher asked why they didn't discuss what could be done about it instead of spending all of their time complaining. They were able to find a way. Shuffleboard, table tennis, and hopscotch were games of great interest to these youngsters, too. The principal, after some persuasion from a very sensible pupil committee, agreed that the school could furnish paint and some equipment. He was still dubious about the advisability of the project because he knew that the play space was badly needed. He feared that it would take the children several weeks to do the job, during which time there would be no play space if rainy days came. After two periods of planning it from every angle, the children decided they would get the eighth grade to help them. With that help the actual work to be done in the playroom could be completed in three days. They did not have the thrill of doing the job alone, but they had the bigger thrill of working with another group. They evaluated this as one of the most satisfying phases of the experience.

Working to improve living in the whole school brings so much satisfaction that when one job is done, children often seek others. When the nurse said to one fourth grade, as she admired their classroom, that she wished the clinic looked as attractive, the children offered to help her improve it. They stenciled a gay butterfly design on lovely yellow curtains. When they were finished in the clinic, the children worked to make the cafeteria a cheerful looking room. Since spring flowers were in bloom, they brought flowers the day they hung the new curtains there. How nice if there could be flowers every day! Could a whole school committee be organized to get fresh flowers each week from the gardens of those willing to share?

The bulletin board outside the cafeteria was chosen as the place for the daily news sheet that told what was going on in the building. At first, the fourth grade wrote this themselves. They missed much of the news, so they eventually saw the advantage of a committee to represent several groups.

The teacher helps children see their own school as a part of a community. He helps them see its relationship to other agencies. He encourages them to find ways of improving existing conditions. However, children's active participation in the living of the larger community comes about because of needs which they feel themselves, in a setting where they can examine many kinds of problems and work with a variety of people.

Some teachers, wishing to secure the participation of children in community affairs and hoping in that way to ensure their continued interest in social issues, center their classroom activities on those problems which seem most significant to the adults of the community. Very often children find these problems extremely interesting. They enjoy investigating live issues. They gain from the exploring they do in the community and from the rich discussions which ensue.

While the results may not always seem significant by adult standards, a much better understanding of their own community and of the social and economic problems of state, nation, and the world can be acquired if children work on problems which they themselves select. They then learn how to recognize problems. They develop standards for evaluating them in terms of which ones make the most significant difference in their own living. They learn to work on problems which seem to be only remotely connected with themselves after they have felt the effect on their own activities of what other classes do. Through firsthand experiences they learn to recognize the widespread implications of interaction among people.

EXTENSION OF INTERESTS

The teacher helps children broaden their general knowledge and at the same time lifts their level of thinking. Through his alertness in searching out and providing experiences, he calls their attention to problems which would not have concerned them previously. Each interest is a springboard to other interests.

Sewer pipes and water lines were being laid in a new housing development. The contractors did not allow neighborhood children on the premises, but the teacher was able to make arrangements with the contractors and every few days took the children over to see and hear what was going on. She began bringing in items from the newspaper which told about the progress being made in the development.

One of these items told of some labor difficulties which seemed to be brewing. Editorials in one local paper stated that the men were asking for too much money. The children watched other papers and brought in items as fast as they appeared. A group of children arranged these clippings on a bulletin board. The children asked questions about the dispute each time they went over to the development. They began to figure rent and food costs and to work out budgets on the salaries the men received.

It was suggested that the children might like to talk to one of the union leaders. They would, and he came over to the group the next time they visited the project. He explained the problems as he saw them. He commented to the teacher on the extreme interest that these sixth grade children had shown. The teacher suggested that the children might like to hear another side of the problem. The contractor said that he would welcome the opportunity to come in, too.

The teacher did not know, when she brought in the first item, that this angle of the housing development would stimulate such deep interest in the problem of how much people are paid, how they get their wages increased, and where the money comes from to raise them. She did not know that this whole matter of contracts and how much the development was costing and how it was being financed would be of vital concern. This interest probably would not have been realized had the teacher not been on the alert to enrich the experiences and broaden the possibilities in the very beginning.

At the same time the teacher introduced the news items she was also introducing other correlated materials. She brought in information on the old Roman aqueducts, and three children took quite an interest in them and on their own read widely the stories of the Gallic Wars, and later shared with the class many of the old Roman legends. Most of the others were fascinated for a short time, but did not show continued interest. She took the class on an excursion to the disposal plant, and there was interest in the way chemicals were added to purify the sewage. The children learned a great deal from looking through the microscope at samples. She introduced some information about the Department of Sanitation. The group, however, was more interested in the microscope, and arranged later to borrow one from the high school science class. While the interests the teacher had envisioned did not materialize, there were a number of valuable outcomes.

Another group of sixth graders had been asked to make a "stained glass" window of parchment paper for the Christmas program and had willingly accepted the assignment but could not visualize such a window, even with all the pictures they could find and with the help of the art teacher. Just how did stained glass windows really look? A tour of several large churches which had unusual windows was arranged. In each church the beautiful windows were admired, and the way they illustrated what had been seen and read was discussed, but busy eyes were seeing strange things they had not seen in their own churches. Here were children of many religions, and each church was strange to some part of the group.

The stained glass windows were finished and not much concern about church architecture or the making of stained glass was shown, even though the teacher suggested taking an excursion to a small factory where stained glass was made. The children were far more interested in a trip to a church of a denomination that they had missed in their tour of churches. It did not have stained glass windows, but they wanted to see the baptistry, about which they had heard from other children.

It was while they were at that church that they saw the organist practicing and heard the exciting sounds which can be made by pushing stops and pressing pedals. So thrilled was the group by this experience that the teacher, even as the group continued to study comparative religion avidly, introduced some experiments

29

with sound and asked the school band leader to demonstrate the way different sounds were produced by several instruments. A small group became involved in the writing of a simple (yet complicated for a group of sixth graders) piece of orchestral music which they used as background when they demonstrated the instruments in an auditorium program given for the fifth grade and for the organist, who had helped.

The interests which the children developed came largely through their experiences together. One experience seemed to lead to another. All along it was necessary, however, for the teacher to help them see the possibilities for going further. By questions and by adding new experiences, she helped them think for themselves.

Children often develop common interests and discover common needs as they go into the community to actually do something together. There was no policeman on the busy street corner near one school. The children had seen smaller brothers and sisters dash across the street in danger of being hit by traffic. Why was there no policeman? They went to the station to ask some questions and to visit the city councilman.

When a group has shown its interest in the community, sometimes community members come to it for help. For example, Duncan's mother asked the teacher in a sixth grade group, which had a sewing machine in its room, if she could come and sew hems on some curtains, as it took her so long to do them by hand. The children said that other mothers might like to use the machine, too. Duncan's mother used it after school. Why couldn't other mothers use it during school hours? Most of them had Thursdays off, and if they used it only after school, only one mother would get to use it each week. If their mothers were there during school hours, they could find out what was happening at the school and would be a part of it. Most of the day it would not matter if the sewing machine made a noise. If they wished to sew during a quiet period, the machine could be wheeled out into the hall. There was really the best light by the hall window anyway. They could leave the machine there all the time. But no, that would not seem so friendly. It would be more pleasant having the mothers in the room. The children publicized the idea in the community, agreeing to show their mothers how to thread the machine, as some had never used one before.

30

Developing Criteria

The development of criteria for judging the value of working through certain problems is a vital part of the selection process. When such problems are selected by the group the teacher can guide but should not dictate or exert pressure to influence the selection. Some limits will be determined cooperatively by both children and teacher. In many classrooms, it will be necessary, because of limits that are placed by the administration or community, for the teacher to explain which activities are permitted and which are not.

The selection process must be directed by the best thinking of which the group is capable. For children, selection is a learning experience and they should be helped to get the most out of it. They should learn not to accept the first suggestions made but to investigate many.

As children proceed with their exploration the teacher helps them develop criteria upon which they can base their judgments. Since a group cannot work on all interests at the same time, it must have some basis for deciding what to focus its attention on. There is a great difference between real interest and idle curiosity. An enthusiasm of one day may be gone by the next or it may grow and still be strong several months later. When whims are accepted as deep interests, a superficial program results. Much of the criticism concerning lack of depth in modern programs has probably arisen because children have not been helped to develop judgment in the selection of areas for study.

One fifth grade worked out some sound criteria. They were not formulated during one period set aside for such activities but over a period of several weeks. When the teacher heard children talking together about the kinds of things they liked to work on she would make such comments as: "That seems to be an important thing to consider. Shall we call it to the attention of the group?" or "That interest didn't last long. I wonder why?"

After they had worked together for several weeks, they summarized the guides they had been developing as follows:

We want to work on something that
  —all of us can agree on.
  —is very important to us.

—will give us other ideas.

—it takes all of us to do well.

—makes it possible for us to learn many new things.

—we can be successful in accomplishing.

—it is possible to find necessary resource material about.

—it will be possible for us to complete in the time we have.

In this incident the teacher watched to see what the children used as a basis for their judgments. He verbalized the values which they considered and called them to the children's attention. They themselves began to watch to see what was actually influencing their decisions. When they became aware that criteria are always used, they saw value in examining them. Then the teacher, through questions and discussion, helped the children think through other criteria which could be considered. They enjoyed seeing what kind of decision each set of criteria would bring.

Once the idea of criteria and their importance is brought to the level of recognition, children continue to develop and refine their understanding of their own individual bases for action and decision. When a group decision is being made they become very critical of those who fail to think through decisions in the light of criteria acceptable to the group. Very often a group asks that the criteria be developed and written down so that all can keep them in mind as the discussion proceeds.

Achieving Skills in Decision Making

A decision that the group will concentrate its chief efforts on one area should be arrived at only after the group has probed its needs. Many times the needs that are stated in the beginning are symptoms of much deeper needs. It is obvious that when boys chase girls about the playground with a snake they are at that moment more interested in teasing girls and getting attention than in finding out all they can about snakes. They may have a general interest in snakes, but they are now using the snake to help them fulfill a deeper need.

A group can live in a rich environment, do much exploring of the resources around them, be concerned with criteria for selection of problems, and still not know how to decide what areas of concern warrant concentrated study. It is easy for both children and teacher to get sidetracked at this point. For example, a group which shows great interest in Indians may have this interest because they find some of the stories about Indians very exciting. Such a group might decide that its needs could best be met through a study of Indians. Actually, they may have very little interest in Indian life as a whole. Perhaps there are other areas of study which would provide still greater opportunities for exciting stories.

It is important that the teacher through his questions help the children consider what kinds of activities would be involved if certain problems were undertaken. Care must be taken that these are the kinds of activities and involve the kind of study to which they are willing to devote a great deal of time.

In helping children select a problem to be tackled by the group, the teacher encourages them to delay final decisions until there is complete agreement. As some children in a group become enthusiastic about an area of exploration, because of their desire to delve more deeply, they may try to influence the whole group to join them. They have ideas for projects which they feel would be very interesting if everyone participated. Sometimes it is the teacher who asks the children what they think about working in some area where he has observed an unusual amount of interest. Children will often clamor, "Let's vote, let's vote," when they see that their ideas seem to be held by the majority. The teacher may talk with them about such a procedure. If they vote, some will be for and some will be against the proposal. "Would it be possible to find something we could all agree on?" Children often feel it would not. The teacher suggests that they try.

At this point, the teacher studies carefully the area or areas in which deepest concern is shown. He searches for additional experiences which could be introduced in these areas in order to provide deeper insights. As more experience is accumulated opinions change, interests shift and become more centralized. New areas may be investigated. Discussions are held almost every day. Finally, the group arrives at a decision. It is built on the experiences they have had. It has come as a result of what individuals in the class were thinking. It involves more comprehensive activity or study than those that the majority had originally pushed. When the decision is finally made, voting is not necessary. One suggestion is built on another and each person's ideas are finer because of the ideas every other person is introducing.

There are many misconceptions about the nature of consensus. Some teachers are now using exactly the same procedures as they did before but instead of saying, "Let's vote," they say, "Let's see what the consensus is," when there is no consensus at all. To others, arriving at a consensus means compromising. They take what all small groups and individuals want and blend it into a subject with which everyone is supposed to be satisfied.

As here used, a consensus is a general agreement on a plan or idea which has evolved from all the ideas of the group, but which may not necessarily feature any one of them in its original form. It goes beyond what any member of the group had in mind.

For instance, a group of seventh graders showed great interest in the development of the cave man. Their questions showed that their interest was a deep one. The teacher brought in pictures of some of the art work that early man had done. Children commented and showed some interest but not great enthusiasm. Stories and books brought the same kind of response and the teacher stopped exploring the area any further. One day, during free period, a heated discussion began, and the teacher hearing the words "cave man" went over to see what was being considered. As she saw where the children's interest lay, she joined in, too. It became evident on questioning that the children were concerned with how the human mind had developed, and that interest in the cave man was so strong because he seemed to represent the beginning of thinking. A discussion with the whole class verified this point, and the group began a period of investigation which lasted several weeks and included, among other things, finding out the physical development of the brain, how superstitions arise and how they are changed, what clinical psychologists do, and ways of relieving pressures in a machine society.

The Teacher's Role in Decision Making

Many teachers who are trying to introduce democratic practices deny children the right to participate in the selection of problems or areas of study. They feel that children are incapable of exercising the kind of judgments which such decisions require. Surrounded as teachers are by the pressing problems of adult life, they are apt to be so concerned with making certain that the younger generation will be better equipped to face the world situation than they themselves were, that they ignore the latest psychological findings. Problems important to children seem secondary to those faced by adults; they are shoved aside in the effort to interest boys and girls in the so-called larger problems.

Teachers often show great indignation when the principal makes decisions that affect them without giving them an opportunity to participate. When parents try to dictate school policies, they become very disturbed. Yet when these same teachers look at the school program they are likely to say, We know what children should learn. They may not see the importance of what we teach them now but they will appreciate it when they grow up. They will soon be adults and must be prepared for life.

Some teachers who deny children the right to participate do it in so subtle a manner that sometimes even they themselves do not know what is happening. Others know very well what they are doing, but they would like to convince the children that they are working in a completely democratic manner. They do this in several ways. If a previous class has engaged in a very fine activity, it seems sensible to speak so glowingly of the advantages which were found in that, that the children are convinced it is also best for them. Thus, there are those classes where year after year chickens are hatched in an incubator or a tea party is given for the mothers or a huge pageant is presented.

If the teacher has a hobby, he may unwittingly influence children to work in that area. A notable example is the sixth grade teacher who, convinced that she was using the best of democratic procedures, was pleased to note that year after year the children expressed a desire to make dioramas of famous American homes.

The teacher may become so impressed with a list of supposed interests which he himself has drawn up that he does not listen to suggestions not in keeping with his own. He sees the adventures of the crusaders as a legitimate area of study, but does not see a present-day revolution in the Near East as worthy of attention.

Other teachers look at the course of study and see what area must be covered. They then subtly lead the children to select that area. They may do it by limiting materials to those in that area. They may do it by the amount of enthusiasm they show when it is mentioned. In either instance, the result is that if the course of study called for Indians, the children choose Indians.

In the examples mentioned above, it is the dishonesty, intended or not, of the approaches that is being questioned. Children's choice is being influenced while an attempt is made to keep them from realizing it. If children do recognize it, then they lose respect for the integrity of the adults who place them in such a position and see the situation that calls for such behavior as unrealistic. If they do not recognize it, they acquire an erroneous concept of freedom of choice and their own capacity to engage in it. In any case, the problems selected are not real ones as felt by the boys and girls, and the quality of learning remains at a lower level than could otherwise be possible.

Even teachers who are working in situations where either the administration or the community limits the kinds of activities which a group of children can undertake may initiate some pupil selection. If such limitations are carefully defined for the children so that they understand the reasons for them, selection of problems by the group within the framework may be very valuable. To face limitations, to work within them, and eventually to stretch them can be an important part of the process.

Summary

In a democratic classroom children must play an active part in selecting the areas in which they will work. The teacher will guide them in identifying and defining needs and outlining experiences through which to meet them, but his most important contribution is in the ways of working he helps them acquire. He shows them how to deepen and broaden their interests through the use of human and material resources. He encourages them to use these resources creatively in seeking answers to their questions.

In addition to helping them find ways of developing and using their environment, he gives them guidance in ways of building criteria to use in making decisions. Through his own way of working, the teacher provides an example. By means of his questions he brings problems to the children's attention, he encourages them to locate and consider the many aspects of their needs, and he directs their attention to analyzing and improving their own process of selection. His effort is mainly toward encouraging the children to think through and improve their ways of working rather than telling them exactly how to work.

CHAPTER III

Planning

All teachers plan. Some write their plans in plan books so that the principal may know what they hope to accomplish and how they will do it. Some scribble their plans on bits of paper which will serve as reminders to themselves during the day. Some do not write their plans at all.

Teachers do both long-term and day-by-day planning. The long-term planning may merely consist of dividing textbook material into nine or ten equal parts, one for each month of the school year. The plan may consist of a list of skills which the teacher checks off as the children learn them; or it may be a series of subject areas which the teacher hopes to cover. It may be a list of children's needs.

The day-by-day planning may consist of a record of page numbers to be covered. It may include drill exercises to be placed on the blackboard, quiet activities for the children, and arrangements for play periods. It may be a schedule of the day's activities, to be printed carefully on a chart.

There are differences of opinion concerning the kinds of planning to be done, who shall do it, and when it shall be done. In determining what their practices will be, teachers often do not examine their philosophy. The type of planning a teacher does may be determined by the kind of planning his own teachers did, by the kinds of reports required in the central office, or by the example set by fellow teachers in the school instead of by a conception of education suitable for a democracy.

Such inconsistency between beliefs basic to our culture and practices prevalent in actual teaching situations is serious for the future functioning of our society. If children are to take their places in a democracy, they must know how to plan for meeting their needs. Children learn to make such plans efficiently when they are involved in some project that is deeply significant to their daily living and when they themselves see the actual relationship of planning to the meeting of their needs.

Even in an autocratic classroom, some provision may be made for planning by pupils. Children are often permitted to plan small, insignificant segments of their work. In many autocratic classrooms a fetish has been made of so-called planning periods. It has become an additional subject in the curriculum. Children, in a bored manner, routinely list the program they will follow for the day. The teacher writes it on a chart in some such words as "We will read. We will do numbers. We will have play period. We will sing. We will go home."

Actually that is not real planning. The children know that there are certain activities they must engage in and that these will go on regardless of the farce of having them plan. Planning done in isolation does not provide the experience children need. Only as they see the relationship of planning to the satisfaction of their own needs will they recognize the importance of it. When they are not involved in the whole process they fail to learn democratic skills.

Some teachers take complete responsibility for pointing out problems and areas of social significance. They then outline the means through which children can work in those areas. When they permit children to plan, they consider the plans acceptable only if they provide for participation in adult activities at an adult level.

This way of working is likely to develop people who cling to problems long after they have become relatively insignificant rather than those who keep abreast of changing conditions. Many people dogmatically take stands on issues and refuse to even look at new evidence that has accumulated through the years, because a teacher told them which stand was the "right" one.

In a situation where orders are handed down by the teacher, children may learn to follow directions, but no matter how much talk there is of democracy they do not become fitted to enjoy its privileges. Usually teachers supervise each phase of the work so closely that the children do not develop skill in interpreting plans. The way of working they learn is actually training them for life under a dictator.

In a democracy everyone participates in over-all planning and takes part in deciding who shall carry out the plans. Even the man on the street is concerned with the kinds of projects government officials recommend and is quick to show his disapproval when the plans do not seem to meet group needs.

Characteristics of Democratic Planning

Planning done by children in the classroom should have the same characteristic as that of adults who strive to live democratically. Plans for meeting the common needs of the group must be made cooperatively, continuously, and thoughtfully. Each of these characteristics is essential if the full benefits of democratic living are to be realized. Each will be examined separately to see why it is important for classroom planning.

PLANNING IS COOPERATIVE

Cooperative planning is important in establishing and maintaining unity. Experimentation shows that a group of people working together can make more effective plans for a group than can be made when only a few people prepare the plans for everyone else to follow. At first such a procedure may seem to be consuming too much time, but the creativity of the ideas produced compensates for the additional time.

When a group is large, it may be necessary to elect representatives to formulate plans. These representatives collect ideas from everyone in the group. Plans made are then presented to the total group for approval. They may find it necessary to come back to the group several times for ideas. Many sets of plans may need to be made before the desires of the group are satisfied.

In many classrooms most of the planning is done by a central planning committee sometimes called a steering committee. This method may succeed very well with adult groups when those involved already understand the principles of democratic planning. Under such an arrangement, however, it is hard for children to feel that they are having a real part in the planning.

In a classroom, the group of children is small enough for all to participate in most of the planning. Sometimes a small committee will be appointed to make plans for one occasion or piece of work. Even then broad policies are made by the total group.

Children gain many advantages by planning cooperatively. They find out what kinds of ideas other members of the group hold. In one rural school, for example, the children were planning the kind of program they would have for their parents. It soon became apparent that group members had different values. Some children felt that dancing was wrong. Hence, they did not wish to include it on the program. Others could not understand why they should think it was wrong. While the planning period was carried on for the purpose of deciding what would be on the program, it gave the children an opportunity to see that all people do not have the same values.

By planning together, children are able to make better use of resources. A teacher may know some things about children's abilities that no child will know, but he cannot know everything about each child that some among thirty children might know. When one group was planning for an exhibit on Italy, David was able to remind Fred that his mother's bedspread was made there. Fred had never noted that label. Such give and take is possible when all the children are showing genuine concern for getting a job done.

Cooperative planning makes possible a high quality of thinking. Every idea presented sets off a chain of other ideas for each group member. Each one who presents an idea feels the thrill of seeing it absorbed into group thinking and is pleased when other ideas develop from it.

One class was playing store. Someone thought they should make play money. Bob thought about his printing set and offered it. Someone else though about organizing a printing company which could make more than money. It took many children thinking together to develop this chain of thought. Individual children each submitting ideas would not have produced the quality of ideas that were developed through group interaction.

When children plan together a feeling of closeness is achieved. They develop an interest in other group members. Human relationships improve. The way in which Miss Anderson's children learned to understand and accept each other illustrates this point.

That class had the reputation of being scrappers, a reputation earned over a period of years. No matter what they attempted, there was always a great deal of discord. An undue number of arguments took place. Despite this, she continued to work with the children on cooperative room ventures. It was in early spring, while they were working together to issue a class magazine that the children themselves began to notice improvement. One of the boys explained it in the following way, "Everything happened to us. It didn't seem as if it would ever be possible to get the magazine done. It's funny, though, because the more problems we had to figure out, the better we got to liking each other. Take me, I'm palling around with kids I couldn't stand last year."

"First we couldn't get the paper. Then they wouldn't let us use the typewriters. Last of all our stencils wore out before we had enough copies. We were determined to have the rest of the kids see that magazine. Every time something happened we put our heads together and did the best planning we could. It took all of us to do it. We get along pretty well now, don't we, Miss Anderson?"

PLANNING IS CONTINUOUS

Work and planning are almost simultaneous. Planning goes on while a need is being defined. There is a concentrated period of planning to begin organization. Planning continues until a task is completed. Through continuous planning, flexibility is achieved. Plans that do not develop as anticipated can be revised until they do work. It is not always possible to foresee what conditions will prevail. If one part of a plan has to be changed, then changes may have to be made all along the line.

As a part of their assembly program, one seventh grade had planned to show some pictures they had made. Two days before the program they found that the equipment available would not project them clearly enough so that they would be seen in the auditorium. Arrangements for other equipment required a great deal of quick planning which could not have been anticipated.

Continuous planning makes it possible to expand plans as action unfolds. If everything is planned in advance, a group can take advantage of the new ideas which the situation itself may demand.

For example, a sixth grade group was studying St. Louis.

During their preliminary planning they listed the places in the city they would like to visit. As they proceeded with their study, however, they revised the list. Many places which had played an important part in the city's early history had been left off the list. The children had no knowledge of these places until they commenced their study. Had hard and fast plans been made in the beginning, the children could not have taken advantage of what they learned along the way.

Resources which were either not available or not known when initial plans were made can be used as soon as they are discovered. The discovery of some old costumes in the principal's closet of one school made it possible to give up the paper ones which had been planned. The paper was then used to make interesting scenery which had not been planned for originally.

Ways of working that are discovered during one phase of the study may immediately be incorporated into the plans and used to facilitate the rest of the work on a project. A small group of children designed hats for the pioneers in the play during their lunch hour. The class decided that if they would divide into groups and each take the responsibility for making some part of the costumes there would be some additional time available for practice. They had not realized the value of committee work when the project started. Now that they had discovered it, they put it to work at once.

When planning is done continuously it is possible to redefine needs as the group works. No matter how careful the definition of a need, the group is likely to discover unforeseen problems. As a result the entire direction may have to be changed.

One group of third and fourth graders changed its plans because of an approaching holiday. The children had been practicing a play in which they enacted an old Indian legend. They had searched the neighborhood for feathers, which they were using on makeshift costumes. The teacher mentioned that it was only three weeks until Christmas. There was still much to do before the play could be presented. If they were to have a Christmas tree or a party, that, too, would take time. They discussed postponing the play, but they did not wish to do that. They did not want to give up Christmas decorations either. At last they decided to do both. They replanned the plot of the play very effectively.

One of the teachers in the building said, "I can't imagine what kind of play you are giving. You collect feathers one week, and the next thing I know you are building a crib for a manger scene. The two activities don't seem to fit together." When she attended the play, she said, "They do fit together. It takes a group of children to do something like that." The play showed a white boy who found an Indian tribe. He enjoyed their ceremonies with them and in turn told them about his Christmas, while the manger scene was portrayed in pantomime. It made a dramatic and thoroughly appropriate performance. The children's needs were met much more effectively through this shift in plans than could have been possible had they been required to carry out original plans.

PLANNING IS THOUGHTFUL

Whether plans are made by an individual, by a few people, or by many, whether they are made by a person or a group in authority and passed down to others or made by a group for its own guidance, thinking is inherent to planning. In a democracy, when plans which concern the whole group are being made, the best thinking of every individual in the group is needed. Everyone is capable of making contributions. Self-confidence must be developed to the point where no one hesitates to express his thoughts. At the same time everyone must be concerned with improving the quality of his own thinking. The impetus furnished by the group awakens and calls forth ideas of which individuals working by themselves would not be capable.

It is the responsibility of the teacher to encourage sharing of ideas. He must recognize growth in thinking so that he can stimulate still better thinking. He must beware of plans thrown together in a hit-or-miss manner. By his own questions he can help children to recognize the superiority of action that follows careful planning.

Initial Planning

After children have selected an area for study or a problem for consideration, there is need for some concentrated initial planning before they begin work. Time spent in initial planning will pay rich dividends in the quality of work that will be achieved later. The thinking which goes into such effort gives children a view of the many possibilities. All of their work will be more meaningful because they see some of the directions toward which it may lead. There is, however, danger of over-planning in the preliminary stages. It may interrupt the dynamic flow of the process. If children are required to plan all the details of how a task is to be done, they may fail to see the need for additional planning.

When children take too long to plan what they are to do, they may become overly impressed with their plans. When some portion of the plans does not work in practice, they may try again and again to make it work. A compulsion to use the plans at hand develops. Progress is delayed because the need for thoughful evaluation is not recognized. Children feel that they have already decided upon this plan as the best. Why should it now be questioned?

Initial planning must be carefully guided so that children can receive the direction they need without unnecessary expenditure of time and energy. Even after they have learned to plan, the teacher must be alert to ways in which they can improve. Initial planning periods should make provision for clarifying purposes, locating specific problems and questions, determining activities, surveying resources, and recognizing limitations. The role of the teacher in guiding each of these will be examined.

CLARIFYING PURPOSES

Children enjoy probing their purposes and feeling the challenge involved in examining them. If they are given adequate help, children can analyze their purposes quite deeply. The teacher, in order to help them achieve skill in doing this, will probably ask questions such as: Just what do we want to do? Why did we decide to work on this problem? What can we accomplish by working together on it that we could not accomplish if each of us worked alone?

Recording the answers on the board so that all the children can see whether or not their own particular concerns are listed there often proves helpful. The teacher continues to encourage them to examine their reasons still further. He may ask why such purposes are important. He may inquire into the meanings of some of their statements. He may point out wider social implications inherent in some of them. Confidence in their own abilities to think is increased as questions bring out ideas they did not know they could produce.

When the probing has gone as far as the children seem able to extend it, the teacher asks whether or not the group wishes to make some statements of purpose by which they can be guided. Intense examination makes it possible for group members to state their purposes much more clearly than before. The teacher calls attention to the resulting changes. A positive feeling toward critical analysis is developed. After they have had a few such experiences, children will themselves look forward to and initiate critical investigation of underlying issues. The amount of probing by the teacher will vary according to the children's age level and background experience.

LOCATING SPECIFIC PROBLEMS AND QUESTIONS

When the children have formulated their purposes, they should seek the implications. Research will be needed so that they can know what activities should be undertaken. The teacher again directs questioning, at least until the children have developed much skill.

The teacher often begins the search with such questions as: What can we ask ourselves about these purposes? What questions come to mind as we think about it? What more detailed problems seem to be included in our larger problem? What areas of study would seem to be fruitful ones? Just as in the clarifying of purposes, the teacher, by means of further questioning, induces a critical examination of each answer given. He may ask, Why should that be included? What can we gain through a knowledge of that? Is this all we need to know? Children soon catch his spirit and begin to question each other.

DETERMINING ACTIVITIES AND SURVEYING RESOURCES

The teacher carries the discussion a step further. If we are to accomplish our purposes what will need to be done? What specific activities will be involved? What kinds of resources will need to be tapped to secure the required knowledge? What skills will be needed if the children are to engage in these activities?

The teacher then helps organize their answers. What must be done first? How can we do that before we have an answer to this? A preliminary plan of action begins to evolve.

Before organizing plans children should know what resources are available. Where can they get written materials? Is the kind of information they need actually included in the materials available? Is it written in a form that they can understand? Where can additional resources be secured? Can they go on interesting excursions? What people can help them?

RECOGNIZING LIMITATIONS

In their enthusiasm over what they are doing, children are likely to outline a program that might take years to put into practice. The teacher should help them estimate the time which various phases of projected plans may require. He may call their attention to the demands made upon their time for other things such as collecting money for milk, play periods, and assembly programs. Holidays sometimes require special preparations and may necessitate halting the work in progress or planning to have it finished by a definite time.

Limits of space may need to be considered, especially if the children are working in a crowded school or in a school with more or less rigid regulations concerning where children should work. The limits of their own ability may need to be considered. If the purpose the group is trying to fulfill is such that there are many ways of accomplishing it, the teacher may not warn about the ability required to follow their plans. Children, discovering how much harder the task is than they had anticipated, will rethink their plans. In many instances, however, when there do not seem to be any ways for the children to achieve desired goals, it seems inadvisable to have them meet complete frustration, at least without warning.

In many schools the kinds of activities teachers and children are permitted to undertake are rigidly limited. In such cases planning can be done in a more restricted manner. The teacher must make clear to the children what the regulations are, whence they have come, and what purpose they are meant to serve. The children then understand which decisions are not theirs to make. Children may doubt the wisdom of some regulations but they are more likely to be willing to continue their planning on another basis. They may work hard to get the regulation removed, or they may decide that it is not important enough to bother with, or that nothing they could do would alter it.

This kind of understanding played an important part with a group of children planning to redecorate its classroom. They wanted to paint the old furniture and make some new pieces. The teacher knew that if they bought paint and applied it, there might be trouble with the Department of Buildings and Grounds. She outlined for the children the problem which was involved, including the need for permission, the channels through which requisitions must go, the possibility of their being turned down, the limited time schedule of the manual arts teacher, and the possible objections to unscrewing the desks in part of the room. Knowing the limitations and the channels which must be used, the children could then decide on a color, study the approved catalogs, make out a requisition, and confer with the custodian and the principal in a more realistic fashion.

Continued Planning

As a group becomes involved in action, much additional planning will be needed. New activities for which plans could not have been made ahead of time will emerge. Provisions must be made so that plans can be made as needed.

Problems that arise from day to day will necessitate some kind of daily planning period. This should not be so routinized that a class must without fail have it at a particular time. On the other hand, there is much in favor of having it scheduled so that children will know when it is appropriate to look to the group for guidance on problems which either have arisen or seem imminent. A desirable way of arranging this is to have a scheduled time when planning will begin but no specified time when it is expected to close. This might preclude such a reaction as one little girl gave. She was asked what they had first period in the morning. "Planning period," was her reply. When asked what they were planning, she answered, "Nothing now, but we just plan anyway until nine-thirty."

There will be times when quite a large portion of the school day will be devoted to planning. Children may work on plans awhile in the morning. Seeing the need for further information they may agree to tackle the problem again later in the day. After checking the availability of supplies or equipment they may reconvene for another session. The intervening activity may be part of the planning even though it does not fit into a formalized procedure. Planning is not just a "let's sit down and talk it over" proposition.

In most groups the first period in the morning is taken as a combined sharing and planning period. It is felt that so much has happened while children were apart during the evening hours that they need time and opportunity to become reoriented to the classroom situation. Many teachers are finding that a longer period of planning in the afternoon, followed by a short period the next morning, is very effective. When plans are made at the end of a day both teacher and children have an opportunity to get supplies and equipment in order. It is also possible to consult out-of-school resources during the late afternoon hours. Parents often are called upon for information or for permission to make an evening visit to the neighborhood library. A committee from one class, accompanied by one of the mothers, went exploring to get needed wood. At a local lumberyard they were able to secure many scrap pieces. The manager agreed to save more pieces for them if they would call for them at a stated time each week. This information made it necessary to make many changes in the day's plans.

Even though the major part of the planning is done in the afternoon, it is almost always necessary to gather for a few minutes in the morning. The experience of the evening will necessitate some changes. Perhaps equipment was not available. The committee cited above had to wait a few days for its wood. As a result several children had to change their proposed tasks for the day.

When a group is working together on a common problem, an unscheduled planning period may often be necessary. The children may remain where they are working if there is some decision to be made which will take only a few minutes. On the other hand, much reorganization may sometimes be needed. The teacher may ask all the children to go to their seats so that the problems can be discussed at length. Any small group may call for such a period. Any individual may suggest the need for it. Or the teacher through alert observation may foresee some difficulties and wish to call them to the children's attention.

On many occasions planning will be done by small groups. The teacher may or may not sit in on these sessions. He stands ready to be of assistance and to call the group's attention to the need for more planning when it seems evident to him. It is done just as it is needed and may not involve more than two or three minutes of consultation. On the other hand, so much disagreement may develop or such difficult problems may arise that work may be stopped for an hour while pros and cons are discussed.

Planning a Working Organization

The past experiences of the children may serve as orientation for developing a working organization. The teacher directs children to realize that their experiences will provide a background in considering ways of working on their present needs. Even though as a group they may not have had experience in working cooperatively, there have been many occasions at school, at home, and in the community where they have planned the organization. The teacher calls their attention to these. For example, there was trouble on the playground last week. How did they organize in order to avert similar disasters? Do the plans seem to be working? How could they be improved?

Some of the children work in the cafeteria. What kind of organization seems to be satisfactory? In what way is that situation similar to their classroom problem? In what ways different? Have any of their families taken long vacations together? What organization preceded such excursions? In planning for birthday parties, how was it possible to keep all the children occupied and happy? Are there any ideas gained from these experiences which will be helped here?

How is their own community organized? The housing development in which they live? On what basis are working groups organized? How do classroom needs differ from these?

The teacher uses the background developed from children's experiences. He helps them see the relationship between jobs to be done and the type of organization needed to do them. He then helps them talk through the various questions and specific problems to be met. The children will examine each approach from many angles. The teacher tries to help them think clearly in terms of practicality, opportunity for constructive working relationships, time schedules, relationships with special teachers and other groups in the building. He checks to see if the organization planned will allow for the emergence of another way of working if this one does not seem satisfactory. He impresses children with the importance of maintaining flexibility. Each new experience will open new avenues for investigation. Each resource consulted provides potential ideas for new resources and new ways of proceeding.

The teacher helps children anticipate difficulties. Foresight may make it possible to avoid some pitfalls. No amount of looking ahead will ward off others. When a group proceeds with full realization that certain difficulties may be encountered, there is not so much discouragement when they materialize. The meeting of such difficulties can result in high quality thinking when everyone is alert and shares in meeting them.

During the organizational planning the teacher is cognizant of the children who do not adjust easily to the group situation. When he sees places where rifts in human relationships are likely to occur, he examines plans to see what provision is being made for these children. Sometimes when a few who are especially vocal appear to be controlling the discussion, he questions others so that their ideas can be considered.

Children learn how to plan as they work to meet their own needs. While they are working on a problem, they are continually developing their ability to deliberate. The teacher must work consciously to develop skills in planning. So important is it that the children learn the kind of planning which requires deep analysis and thought that the teacher must not depend on their learning merely through his example.

By means of his questions, he must stimulate them to create the kinds of plans which will fit the situation. He pushes children's thinking, directing them to analyze their own purposes and recognize the limitations of their own abilities and the situation. When children begin to feel the depth of thinking they are attaining, he helps them analyze the reasons. He strives at all points to help them assume an ever-increasing amount of the responsibility for doing the analyzing. In this way he moves children from superficial to more careful planning.

CHAPTER IV

Activating Plans

Those who have misunderstood the purposes of democratic procedures in a classroom have sometimes thought that the children are expected to do very little work. But when teachers are thoroughly grounded in democratic philosophy and are using it as the basis for the educational program the children work harder than when class organization is rigid.

Means used for stimulating children's efforts and ways of working will differ according to the situation. In an authoritarian school there may be some opportunity for cooperating in areas such as singing and dramatics, but most of the time children will be expected to work alone. Sharing ideas or helping one another gain knowledge or learn basic skills is likely to be discouraged or not permitted at all. The children are encouraged to outshine each other in the class. Much of their thought will be concentrated on showing how smart they are.

Where group process is being used, children will work together in many areas. Sometimes a group of children working together accomplishes more than could be done if they worked as individuals. Sometimes, however, the concentrated attention of one person is required. Whether a child works individually or in a group will depend on the nature of the work to be done.

Much of the children's attention will be given to improving the conditions of group living. They will put forth their best efforts because of their deep interest in the group project. Feelings of success will develop as a problem which has importance to the children is being met satisfactorily. They are able to sense the improvement which results in their own living.

Children do not spend all their efforts on improving group living. Each individual works also to improve his own knowledge and skills. In a democratic situation, however, children work on skills for which they, themselves, feel a need. As they work on problems, they find themselves in need of tools for working. The desire to learn comes from within each child.

Flexibility—the Keynote

Some teachers feel that unless a class is split into small groups or committees, real cooperative work cannot go on. They therefore quickly divide their children into committees and ask each committee to choose a subject for study, or they assign a subject. When a group is working democratically, however, organization is planned so that common needs can be met in the most intelligent manner possible. Committees are not formed for the sake of committees, but so that certain tasks which can be done better by small groups can be accomplished.

COMMITTEES

A committee functions as an organ or a group. Just as the heart is part of the body and responds to the feeling of the whole organism, so a committee is part of the whole group and works so closely with it that it can carry out the wishes of all.

The number of children on a committee may fluctuate as the size of the task increases or diminishes. Sometimes a child may be a member of more than one committee. Sometimes two committees may merge. When a class is preparing to solve a problem or do a piece of work, small groups are organized when there is work to be done. When the particular task assigned is completed a committee is dissolved.

In some classrooms there is no definite meeting time for committees. There are large blocks of time set aside as work periods. Committees meet during this time for as long as they need to work together. On some days, some committees may not meet at all. Other groups may find it necessary to meet during the entire work period and even come in early the next morning in order to finish a report which another group is waiting for.

In classrooms which must operate under a rigid schedule, most of the committees may have to meet at the same time. In such situations it will be necessary for the teacher to check briefly with each committee on what its plans for the day include and to make further suggestions to facilitate their work. The work of one committee may be needed immediately. The teacher may help there. Another group may be having difficulty in doing the job it has mapped out. He may help it replan or develop the skills it needs. Sometimes disturbed, restless children cause trouble in a group. The teacher may sit in on such a group in order to decide whether reorganization of group structure is needed or whether the group has veered away from the original need that was felt by the children.

Children who have not worked on committees will need the teacher's help frequently. To organize a group of children and send them away to work without offering them an opportunity to at least test their plans is a mistake. Children often feel helpless under such circumstances and become discipline problems. Even committees of children with long records of experience profit from having someone who can help them make a more searching evaluation of their ways of working than it is possible for them to do by themselves.

When a committee is first organized the whole group may suggest ways of working and resources. Then after the new committee has had a few minutes to explore possible approaches, the teacher helps it map out a way of beginning. With younger classes the teacher will need to stay rather close at hand even after they have gained experience. He must make certain that they develop work habits which make it possible to do the kind of thinking needed for problem solving.

A small group may or may not select a chairman. Much depends upon the nature of its task. If the group is likely to be in existence for a period of time it may be helpful to have someone who coordinates its efforts. The leadership may shift as the nature of the work changes. All committees do not need to have the same kind of working arrangements.

Places of committee meetings will vary according to what the goals are. They may be in the hall, in the principal's office, in the library, or in their own classroom. They will be where the job can be done well and still fit into the total situation. When a classroom is filled with screwed-down seats, children very frequently do most of their group work at the front and the back of the room.

Very often committees will engage in quite comprehensive research in order to develop the background and information needed to make necessary decisions before they proceed further. In classrooms where, because of curriculum restrictions, the teacher has had to limit children's work to the study of problems within a prescribed area, all the children will be engaged in research, but the research will be designed to throw light on problem areas that the children themselves have outlined.

REPORTS

Since an entire group is involved in working on a problem, it has an interest in the activities of each of its subgroups. But formal schedules for committee reports are not always practicable. A committee should report only when it has something to report or when it needs the help of the larger group.

Reporting can be done in many ways. It should not be a formal answer to a parrot-like question, Which committee is ready to report? asked in a stilted voice by a chairman who has no genuine interest in what is to be said, but has learned that when he asks that particular question, someone will rise and report.

When there is unity in a group, there is a sensing together of who is ready to report and what reports are needed. Reporting becomes an informal give and take of information and suggestions. Sometimes a teacher may say, "We can't go any further until we have heard from the ——— committee." Or sometimes a group will say, "We have some very interesting findings which we think could be of help to the rest of you." Sometimes a complete report will not be given to the total group. The committee will simply recommend action and then move on to study a new phase of the problem. In some cases the showing of a completed project such as a map with a few well-chosen comments concerning the difficulties in portraying that particular bit of knowledge and suggestions for its use may be the extent of a committee report. In other cases it may involve a very detailed report.

Informal progress reports may be called for almost daily during the planning period as the teacher checks to see what help is needed. Two or three sentences from a group spokesman will suffice for that. If the teacher observes some overlapping, he may ask each group to report more fully so that they may redirect their courses if necessary. Similarly, if he suspects gaps, he checks to see whether the problem under question is being solved.

RECORDS

Some groups keep very comprehensive records of what is being done; others keep very sketchy ones. Whatever records will help them to meet their needs most effectively, to keep their work flowing most freely, are the ones that should be used. Some teachers try to plan in advance exactly what kinds of records will be kept. In many instances children do not feel a need for them or they may not understand their use. As a result, many class logs are sterile and worthless. They are a stereotype rather than an actual account of what is happening in the class. Teachers force children to keep them and both teachers and children consider them a nuisance. Records merely imposed for the purpose of keeping records are dull and lifeless. Children will, however, require the teacher's guidance in recognizing the need for records. Sometimes a group plans many more things than it can manage. The teacher points out that records would help them remember what needs to be done.

When the children begin to plan what kinds of records will serve them best they will look about to see how other people keep records. The teacher makes many suggestions. They may try several kinds. They learn, through using them, which are helpful. They find out that the kind of records which are helpful in one situation may not be in another.

A group develops appreciation of records when it is ready to make a comprehensive evaluation of progress. It can easily see how its ways of working have improved. Children note, too, that what they considered important for the record in the beginning no longer seems so important. Their values have obviously changed. The records make it possible for the group to analyze how it began work and on what basis it has chosen its areas for study. Records show how decisions were made and to what extent they were carried out.

CULMINATION

Action of the group should lead to fulfillment of the need felt by the group. In order that the principal, teachers, and parents may know what is going on, there is sometimes a tendency to channel all action toward a large group activity known as a culminating activity. It is perfectly possible that such an activity, for example, the production of a play, may meet the needs of the group. But it is also possible that pointing the action toward a culminating event may make the plans so inflexible that only superficial needs can be met. Not all needs, however, are worked on in a way that will permit a big closing event. If satisfactions are achieved through doing a job without making a spectacular showing, there is no reason for manufacturing one.

Sometimes children do wish to share their results with others. They want their friends or parents to see what they have done. The decisions of what they will present, who shall be invited, and when and under what conditions become a part of the whole learning process. For someone to say that each class must have a play twice a year presupposes that without such a rule there would be no plays at all. Many things children would really like to do are not done because there are so many things they are required to do. "Of course we are tired of this unit," said one teacher, "but you know how it is—we still have to think of some way to culminate the work." Had he thought about it, he would have realized that the unit had culminated already, that it had died long ago. Just as a piece of work begins with a need, it ends when the need has been met. But those who think of the curriculum as units of work, each with a beginning and an end, may lose that valuable experience when, weeks or months later, the group may proceed with another angle of the study.

SUBJECT MATTER

As they work together to meet their needs, children delve deeply into the subject matter of history, geography, literature, science, mathematics, and the arts. They accumulate vast stores of knowledge as they study the problems which they face in their daily living. Seldom, however, is any one of these subjects approached in the so-called logical manner in which it has traditionally been presented to children. Rather it is drawn from many sources as required.

The subject matter used in a classroom should relate to the problem being considered. The content will vary from classroom to classroom since the needs of no two groups are exactly alike.

Children and teachers search cooperatively for the knowledge that is needed. Teacher guidance is important because children do not have a broad view of the kinds of information available. As children grow older they learn to make a better and better selection of subject matter.

The experience of past generations should be used when an understanding of their problems is helpful in meeting present-day situations. Thus history is not studied in a vacuum nor are historical facts stored away so that children may participate in quiz-kid programs. Children who have made use of history often develop an interest in it. They learn more history than they would be expected to acquire in a conventional history course.

SKILLS

As the children work, the teacher keeps his eyes open to see what skills they need. Skills are learned when a need for them is felt. Children do not learn skills in general, but skills to use in specific situations. The teacher helps them to recognize a need for skills and to acquire them when they can be used. Later, children are given help in refining their skills. As the level of their goals becomes higher, their need for skills is greater and they learn new ones and refine those they already have. As one boy said, "In the other school I went to there were two important things—reading and no gum-chewing, and if you couldn't read you were thrown out of class, and if you chewed gum, too. After having reading all day you didn't like reading when you got home because you were tired of it. Here I read every chance I get and at home, too, even though nobody makes me. It's fun now."

The teacher may suggest ways in which the children can improve what they are doing. A lettering pen will help Jerry put a finishing touch on his scrap book; Susan does not know about margins; Raymond has not discovered the gold paint in the cupboard. The teacher suggests that Alice enlarge her picture collection and send it abroad in exchange for some from another country. Alice organizes a small group to help. How shall they classify the pictures? What additional kinds should be included? The whole class gives suggestions and many contribute pictures.

Grace has written a story about her pet chicken. It is a wonderful story, the first one Grace has done. She reads it to many of

57

the children. The teacher shows her how to sew covers on some folded pages. Now her story is in a real book. She illustrates each page. The front page says "A Pet Chicken—Written and Illustrated by Grace Jones." Thus, practice in reading is done voluntarily.

Not all children will learn the same skills and knowledge, but each will acquire learnings that are rich and diversified. The accumulation of knowledge for its own sake is not the primary purpose of the school. In each case, learning takes place because the child feels a need for it. Children feel a need for many skills, often more than adults expect of them. New techniques in art which would make their backdrop look more colorful were quickly developed by members of one group when this skill was needed. Long rambling sentences almost disappeared when one group of fourth graders put out several issues of a class newspaper and did long hours of careful planning of headlines which were short but packed with meaning.

The teacher has a responsibility to encourage children to increase their skills in many areas. He looks ahead to see what new skills will probably be needed and is ready to give help when such needs materialize. One teacher found the children in need of skill in counting by two's and four's. They were making play money because Billy and Joe had set up a temporary block structure and labelled it "general store." With a yardstick they began measuring off large sheets of paper. "Four, eight, twelve, sixteen, twenty," they counted as they marked the length. "Two, four, six, eight, ten, twelve, fourteen," they counted as they marked the width. Other children took up the refrain. The children helped them carry on as far as 100—just because it was fun. The teacher encouraged them and on another day asked them if they still remembered how it was done. The children were proud of their new skill.

The teacher also helps children with discussion techniques. As they become necessary, they are practiced. Sessions are not held so that children will learn the technique, but because there is something that needs to be talked out. Sometimes, children try to see who can talk the loudest, or someone wins his point because he is very persistent. The teacher is alert to a need here for guidance. He helps them see how things could have been said more effectively. Children soon learn to do this for themselves.

As one child put it, when they were evaluating a discussion period, "What we said was good; the way we said it was not good."

Children learn to be good leaders of discussions because they have been members of groups where others have led well and have themselves had an opportunity to conduct discussions which were important to them. They learn that sometimes plans for discussion progress well and at other times they do not. If what they want to present is important to them, they are glad to receive help and even seek it. Merely making a theoretical study of discussion techniques does not produce skill in that area, but practical experience with careful guidance does.

The teacher helps children with skills of reading and writing. The kind of help he gives will vary from child to child. The story of Jimmy, a fourth grader, illustrates how individualized some of this help must be. Jimmy had always insisted he did not want to write. His teacher did not force him. One day she saw him at the typewriter, picking out letter after letter. Often, he spoke to someone near him, asking how to spell a word. It took him one and one-half hours but he wrote a long letter to a college supervisor who often visited the room. The form for the heading was fairly well done and the salutation was in the proper place. There were no capital letters and no punctuation marks. The letter told what had been going on at the school, and while there was no paragraphing, the organization of material was good.

The next day, Jimmy was at the typewriter morning and afternoon. He wrote a two-page, single-spaced letter to his mother and father. It had the same characteristics as his earlier letter. The spelling was all right because he asked about the words he did not know. When on the third morning he started another letter to the college supervisor, the teacher sat down beside him and showed him how to make capital letters, and explained that whenever you start with a new idea you begin with a capital letter. This information appealed to Jimmy, and since his sentence structure was good, his capital letters almost all went into the right places.

Day after day, Jimmy took his place at the typewriter. The other children evidently understood this streak of letter writing, as they showed no surprise, and no one questioned his right to be there on many successive days. One day the teacher showed him how to put in periods and question marks. Another time she explained paragraphing. Each time he listened with interest and showed by the way he applied what he heard that it all made sense and seemed useful.

Jimmy had taken active part in many room projects where it had been necessary to write out programs, invitations, letters, and stories, but he always managed to get someone else to do the writing. After eight days at the typewriter, during which time he wrote some letters that an adult might claim with pride, he stopped writing for his own pleasure, but wherever, as a member of the group, there was a need to write something, he no longer hesitated, but worked painstakingly to do a good job.

In less than two weeks after his letter writing spree he asked the teacher if she would like to have him read a story to her. Jimmy had often looked at books and many times he had dictated his own stories to the teacher, so that he had several volumes of his creative work, but he had never shown an interest in reading them to himself or others after they were written. Now he came, not with a pre-primer, but with a second grade reader, and read the story well. He continued to read to anyone who would listen and even went into the first grade room to read to those children. Soon he was reading *The Five Chinese Brothers*. As he got into more difficult books, there were words he did not know. The teacher at first told him the words. As he showed an alertness in recognizing new words, she gave him some techniques in word recognition. Before the year was over, he was taking books home. He read *The Story of Kit Carson* and many other books which were on fourth and fifth grade levels.

It was three months after his experiences at the typewriter that he began to write stories in manuscript. It seemed hard for him but he stuck at that for many days, just as he had stuck at the typewriter. The teacher helped him learn the correct way to make the letters.

All children will not learn to read and write in the way Jimmy did. Jimmy was slow in developing. Had he received more meaningful stimulation, however, he might have learned these skills at an earlier age. A program which is concerned with meeting the needs of each child is so arranged that teachers are able to give help as the children can use it. The teacher works differently with each child as he gives help in skills. He varies his procedures according to the background of the child.

Skills may be needed in using reference materials. The children may not even realize that such materials are available. The teacher calls their attention to the library card catalog, to the World Almanac, and other materials. The teacher may arrange with the operator of the filling station to furnish maps for planning the route the school bus should take on an excursion so they can see as many things as possible on the way.

Among the many important learnings that children will acquire, will be skills in communication, in fact-finding, in using mathematical concepts; appreciation of people, nature, and the arts; understanding of social problems; and the self-respect which allows creative experimentation. These will be learned because they contribute directly to a more effective meeting of needs and to the development of persons capable of a high level of cooperative action. Children go into these areas deeply when they need to solve problems. They must read and write if they are to gather and make use of important data. It is unnecessary to sugar-coat any of these rather complicated skills. Seeing an honest need for them, children will work to master them.

Through studying the progress of many class members, it is possible to see what areas and what specific skills within those areas are needed by several children. In addition to spending time with individual children, the teacher may organize a group, saying, "Some of us will be working on addition of fractions this morning. If you need help why don't you join us."

The teacher keeps a careful record of each child's progress in many skills. He may say, "Jerry, I notice that you are getting along fine with your division. Why don't we push those skills of yours a bit further this morning?" He may say to the class, "I notice that many of us are having some difficulties with quotation marks. Within the next few days we should plan a period when we can study their use."

When children have already had much need for a particular skill and have seen it used again and again, a small amount of instruction will usually suffice. Where more is needed the teacher must arrange such help. Children often become very discouraged when they do not have the skill to do the things they wish to do.

Children may be satisfied with haphazard skills unless the

teacher emphasizes careful work habits. Many children are disgusted with their work and with school in general without knowing why. Muddling along without skillful guidance in locating difficulties and without help in overcoming them is frustrating to most children.

This does not mean that the teacher insists on identical sets of skills for all children. If need for a skill is not felt by the children, both teacher and children waste time if they try to develop it. Under such circumstances, children are likely to become even more frustrated than when they have been given too little help. Skills that would take hours of drill to master can often be learned in a few minutes after a child has developed insight into their uses.

Daily Program

Every school day should be different, designed by the children to meet their needs on that particular day. Children do need some kind of framework within which to work. When there is no schedule they do not know how to make their own plans. How can they know when to bring in materials if they do not know when there will be time for them to work? How can a committee wait until a planning period to receive suggestions for its work if there is no certainty of such a period? Children appreciate the opportunity to extend a period or to change its place on the program. They do not, however, like to work completely according to the impulse of the moment. For example, some activities are more noisy than others. Children should not be required to do all of their studying to the accompaniment of the hammers in another part of the room. Some activities require specific teacher help. Time should be scheduled for that.

A program that is divided into a few large blocks of time is more flexible than one in which a special time is listed for every task the children will be doing. When children have an hour or an hour and a half which is not specifically scheduled they can plan, when planning is needed. Reports can be followed with action. Individual committees are able to accomplish a great deal. Much time is wasted when the whole class must move from one activity or area of study to another every few minutes. No sooner are materials out and ready for use than they must be put away.

Eventually children feel the futility of getting them out at all and as a result do less pretentious and less creative planning. When time is very rigidly scheduled it is difficult to make use of a wide variety of resources. Books are about all that lend themselves to such quick-change tactics. With them, too, the fewer used, the less there is to get out and put away.

Both daily and weekly programs should be planned cooperatively by teacher and children. At the beginning of the year the teacher should work out with the children a list of the kinds of activities which they may wish to carry on. They can experiment with ways in which to use their time to best advantage. They change their schedule frequently until they are able to arrive at a practical framework.

The very flexibility of daily programs makes it difficult to give illustrations. Two teachers have found the following arrangements helpful:

Schedule I

[This program was used in a fourth grade where teacher and children were free to arrange the schedule that seemed best for them.]

9:00-10:30	Planning time and work period
10:30-11:00	Play (outside or in gym)
11:00-12:00	Working to improve skills
12:00- 1:00	Lunch
1:00- 1:45	Quiet time
1:45- 2:30	Arts—music, painting, drama
2:30- 3:00	Story time

The large block of time in the morning made it possible for the children to use as much time for planning as was needed. By nine o'clock many of the children were in the room with their materials spread out ready for work. After a short time together they could continue without having to put everything away.

The eleven o'clock period was really a continuation of the work period. The teacher did, however, during this period help individuals or small groups with skills. Sometimes a full class session was held. Of course, the teaching of skills was not confined to this period. The teacher was busy with that during the work period, too, but there was other time for practice.

The quiet period at one o'clock was for children who wished to rest or lie down. It provided time for additional independent reading. Some children wrote stories. Others painted pictures. Painting was almost always done by some children during the morning work period too. It was felt, however, that because much of the time they were so very busy on jobs that concerned the whole room, there should be a special time when they could express themselves creatively.

SCHEDULE II

[This schedule was used in a fourth grade where the teacher was expected to plan a specific time for the usual school subject areas.]

9:00-10:00	Social Studies
10:00-10:30	Art or music
10:30-10:45	Play
10:45-11:15	Science
11:15-12:00	Mathematics
12:00- 1:00	Lunch
1:00- 2:00	Reading
2:00- 2:40	Language
2:40- 3:00	Spelling and writing

By using this schedule in a flexible way the children were able to work freely. The period before play was used for planning and for working on special problems chosen by the children. The children, however, were restricted in their choice to subject areas listed in the state courses of study. Each fourth grade in the district was expected to "cover" that material. Their time in the social studies was spent in research, reporting, and discussions. Sometimes there were dramatizations or puppet shows.

Having the art and music period immediately following made it possible to dove-tail the two periods in such a way that the children really had one long work period. The whole afternoon became a language arts period. The children found time to do much creative writing. Any quiet activities of the morning could be very easily continued in the afternoon. Despite the limitations which seemed to be placed upon her, the teacher felt fairly unrestricted as she helped children grow in their use of group process.

The teacher helps children develop skill in organizing to carry out their plans. He helps them in finding ways to break up into smaller groups. He encourages them to make use of records. He assumes the responsibility for acquainting them with many skills and helping them learn them as they are needed.

CHAPTER V

Evaluating

People are evaluating all the time. They evaluate when they say, "We like this, we don't like that." Some people make decisions impulsively without giving much thought, if any, to alternative actions or to the implications of their decisions. Others consider a question carefully before arriving at a decision. Some accept values from those around them without making any attempt to develop a consistent set of values for themselves.

Many teachers agree that adults should do their own evaluating but feel that children are too young to know when they need help. They feel that children have no way of judging when a way of working is effective. Hence, most schools have had teachers evaluate children and their work. Children solve arithmetic problems and the teacher checks the answers. They study a chapter in history and are given a test to find out how much they have learned. At the end of the year an achievement test is given so that adults can decide whether they can do the work of the next grade.

Since children will be expected to form their own judgments when they become adults, they must learn how as children. They need to learn how to evaluate their own progress, to recognize which ways of working make progress possible for them and to decide what can be done to improve their relationships.

If relationships with the adults close to children are satisfying, they are likely to adopt many adult values and to base their decisions on them. If they resent the way adults treat them, they may reject their value systems and develop one not at all adaptable to harmonious relationships with other people. In either case they are not operating on a firm base which they themselves have developed out of their own experience.

In the last twenty years there has been a trend away from the narrow concept of evaluation as testing achievement to a broader concept of it as progress toward a set of goals. At the same time, however, although children have been encouraged in some instances to evaluate their own progress, usually children have known even as they did it that unless their judgments concurred with those of the adults in the situation, theirs would not be permitted to stand.

To develop the ability to make effective judgments, children must learn by judging things that are important to them. If children recognize the significance of carefully considered evaluations and gain skill in making them, they will be able throughout the rest of their lives to continually improve the quality of their living. In learning this skill, they must have help. Just as in the other basic elements of the group process, teachers must assume responsibility for making such learning possible.

Evaluation Is Continuous

Evaluation is not an examination coming at the end of a long process. It goes on during the entire process. Hence children will evaluate while the need is being defined and during the planning and action which result. If it were left to the end, then the help gained from it would not be available for meeting the current need. For example, a troop of Boy Scouts in planning for their spring jamboree set up a schedule of duties. As soon as the first meal was over, it was obvious that some committees had practically nothing to do while others were overworked. This was discussed at the evening session and as a result a readjustment was made. If the evaluation had been left until the trip was over, group living could not have proceeded smoothly.

In most cases it is not necessary to schedule a regular time for evaluation. In fact, it is seldom advisable. There is something frightening about having what they have done examined so formally by the group. Usually more can be accomplished if the teacher encourages evaluation at times when the children's feeling of satisfaction can be increased by so doing. As with the definition of need and planning, teachers will rely upon questions. When children are exploring, the teacher may ask, "What is so fascinating about that book? Do you like it better than the one you had yesterday?" A simple comment such as, "Then I wonder if that doesn't give us some help in selecting books which will appeal to you? Perhaps we can go to the library tomorrow to see what they have that meets your standards?" helps focus children's attention on evaluation.

A group of second grade children was putting away its dress-up clothes. The teacher commented, "You've had so much fun today. What's so special about playing hospital?" The children were able to work through a fairly well-developed analysis of the factors which make for quality in dramatic play periods.

Coming in from play the teacher may mention that this seemed to be the best play period they had had in months. What made it so? What can be done to ensure more like it? In this way the teacher is encouraging the evaluation of human relationships.

When a group is attempting to arrive at some decision concerning what common problem they will attempt to study together, the teacher will help examine each interest which has been shown. Here he can ask, "How do we know that this is important?" "Where did we get it?" "How did that group happen to develop such an interest?" "Have we really considered everyone's needs as we made our selection?" "How can we be sure of that?" He is helping children arrive at a decision through thoughtful evaluation.

"How shall we know whether or not our plans were well made?" This is a challenge that may well be given to an intermediate age group that is launched on a new endeavor. This will lead to a constant evaluation as the plans are put into practice.

Classroom routines are subject to surveillance. When the children sense the improvement that can result from a few simple changes, they are alert to suggest that it is time they examine their ways of working. When one work period seemed noisy and disorganized, a committee came to the teacher. "Don't you think it is time for us to stop and plan a little more carefully so we'll all know where we are going?" they asked.

After spending several periods planning the scenery for its play, another group found that no one wished to work on it. Instead of berating them the teacher asked them to consider why.

How had they arrived at the decisions they had? Was it that they didn't want a play? That not enough searching had been done to get creative ideas for the scenery? Where in their planning had they short-circuited? In each instance through the interjection of questions the teacher helped children develop their own way of evaluation.

When a group has finished an activity or accomplished something worth-while, they want to talk about it. They do not want a stereotyped, stuffy discussion. Rather they wish to share ideas on "how we did." Although the teacher cannot dictate what children will accept and absorb from an experience, he can help them verbalize the things they do accept. The teacher should then help them analyze the reasons for their choices.

Sometimes a teacher will ask a group of children what they have learned. Unless they have been working together democratically for some time, their answers will probably be almost entirely in terms of content. The teacher lists these on the board. He presses for as many as the children can give him. When they seem to have exhausted their ideas, he may ask if they do not think it is an impressive list. What made it possible for them to learn so many things? How much do they know about each one? They did not set out to study all these things. Which ones did they have specifically in mind when they started? Whence came the others? Why was this knowledge important to them? How much of it do they think they will be able to recall the next time it is needed?

This is the direction questioning might take as children examine the way they worked together. How *did* they come to learn all these things? Did their way of working have anything to do with it? What was it about their way of working which made this possible? What have they learned about ways of working which will help them with the next problem? Will this same process be helpful in out-of-school situations? Should they be listed among the learnings gained?

Sometimes these questions are asked when the group faces a new problem or begins a new activity. How shall they work? How have they worked before? Which procedures succeeded? Which did not work well? One group did not succeed in getting the school board to provide funds for the improvement of the playground. When they visited the President of the Board, he asked significant questions which the children could not answer intelligently. Why did they not have these facts at their fingertips? Why did they not foresee some of the problems involved? Where did the method of working break down?

In this way the teacher stimulates children to ask questions and encourages them to think through their answers before starting a new project. Another way in which the teacher sets evaluation in motion is to help children find signs of improvement which have occurred in their group living. How did their approach to things contribute to the new satisfactions they are feeling? What decisions sensibly arrived at have made life better for everyone? The teacher helps bring to the surface for analysis the deep feeling of unity which a group develops as it works and plans together.

Teachers must be careful not to be satisfied too easily. When a class project succeeds it is easy to leave unrecognized the opportunities which existed for doing even better. Children sometimes will see lacks in areas not emphasized by the teacher. It is important that the standards used in evaluation be arrived at and used cooperatively if the highest level of achievement is to be attained.

One teacher was quite pleased with a play given by the children in her room, yet the children were dissatisfied. The teacher was using such criteria as whether or not the play pointed out a moral, how quietly the scene shifting was done, and the artistic merits of the lighting effects. The children had for their criteria the way other children in the school liked the play and the satisfactions they themselves felt from participating in it. Cooperative work linked with cooperative evaluation as the play was being practiced would have eliminated or greatly reduced the conflicting evaluations.

Sometimes a group can be helped to evaluate its own program if it visits a class in another school. Spending a day in someone else's room has often given children much insight which they could use in interpreting their own programs intelligently.

From time to time the teacher helps individual children analyze the changes which have taken place in their own behavior. They note that many conflicts of the past disappeared through working with others on a common problem. They understand each other better than they did before. As children gain status with others, their respect for themselves improves. Emotional reactions against others become less frequent as they become working members of the group. Through such analyses children become experts in group dynamics, even though they may never have heard the term. They learn how to include children who would normally be left out. It is easy to include them when they are needed.

Through their own interest in improving the process and through the satisfactions they gain as they are able to improve it, children learn to make use of evaluation as a means for improving their way of working. The following illustrations show how quickly children begin to recognize the value of such practices.

The carnival went off all right, but it would have been better had they been organized to take care of the crowds. What could have been arranged? Why was not this difficulty foreseen? Thus one class analyzed and began an evaluation of a school project.

To a small group that was working on a mural together, one boy said, "I think this needs a group decision. I don't think we can go any further until we ask the others."

When planning the Mother's Day Tea, one girl in the fourth grade said, "We'll have to do more planning for this than we did for the Easter play." In another room, a girl was heard saying, "I believe we are making up our minds too soon. Do we really have enough evidence? Are we sure that the information we do have is accurate? I don't believe we should decide what to do until we have investigated much more. How can we act intelligently if we don't study the whole idea carefully?"

The third grade from a neighboring school had spent the day in Massey School and another third grade from the same school was coming in two weeks. "Let's talk about today's visit," said Juanita, "so that when the next group comes we won't make the same mistakes." In general, things had gone well, but, as one girl declared, "there seemed to be a kind of emptiness." They analyzed the way they had worked when the guests were there. They decided that when the next class came, they would do something together that was important to all of them. They decided that eating was important. They would make ice cream in three freezers. George's mother would come to help.

A group of third and fourth graders who had visited La Guardia Airport was told by the guide that he was impressed by the freedom with which they asked sensible questions. He said that in many of the groups children either couldn't think of questions or seemed afraid to ask them. The teacher later recalled the incident and asked why the guide had said this. Frank, who had come from another group several months before, answered, "Kids in this class don't sit at desks and read books all the time. We talk things over. It's not just pouring work in. Maybe the other kids are afraid to ask questions for fear their teacher will holler at them for asking something silly."

One third-grade boy said, when Valentine's Day was approaching, and the children were deciding how they would observe it, "We'll be satisfied with just a little. We have so much else to do." "Yeah," answered another, "we have bigger things to do."

In each of these instances children have recognized the importance of process. It has become so important to them through weeks of being encouraged to examine it that they themselves initiate discussion of it.

Awareness of Democratic Process

To what extent are children using the democratic process in meeting the problems of everyday living? This question concerns every teacher who is attempting to help children develop skill in using the process. An even greater concern, however, is the extent to which children recognize the process as the basis for a way of life.

Children may be working together very well. They may be realizing many benefits from their work together. Still some of them might feel that they are not learning so much as they should. Previous school experience has given them an idea that school is a place where facts must be memorized and number combinations drilled. It is important that they recognize what they are doing as of basic importance not only in their living today but in their living tomorrow as parents and citizens.

It is possible that if children do not really understand what makes life satisfying for them they may allow someone with dictatorial tendencies to curtail their way of working before they can realize what has happened. Or, in the rush of busy living they might drop some of the elements of the process and, as they do, it will become weakened and eventually disappear. When many individuals understand the significance of the process, goals of the large group are achieved more effectively. Those who under-

stand it can explain it to others. Teachers can do this by helping children deepen insights in the way described earlier in this
chapter.

To those who do not understand democracy at work, it might
appear that the development of the individual is neglected as he
becomes involved in working for the group. This, however, is far
from true. As children make their own contributions and recognize their importance in group thinking, as they see the impetus
which their ideas give and feel the effect which they have, their
estimation of themselves improves. This helps them develop a
positive approach to life. They are inspired to continue working
at a progressively higher level. The skills which each individual
must continue to improve in order to work with the group are a
help to him in satisfying his individual needs. As his concept of
himself is lifted, the quality of his living improves. Working to
improve himself would not be nearly so effective or half so
satisfying as the progress he makes with a group.

As children themselves recognize the importance of the process,
they will be able to interpret it to the community. The teacher
helps children meet criticisms which may be made of their way of
working. He also helps them assume part of the responsibility
for interpreting the process.

In one community parents were being quite vocal in their
criticisms of "modern" practices in the schools. The teacher of
one class asked the children why this was so. They listed the
things that parents were criticizing. To the children some of the
things seemed superficial and relatively unimportant. They decided to list the things they regarded as important about the way
the school, and especially their own room, operated. They thought
that parents surely would not object to the purposes they had in
mind, the learnings for which they were working. The lack of
approval must have stemmed from lack of knowledge of why
things were being done.

The children decided to construct a series of slides which
would show how their group worked democratically together and
what was accomplished as a result. Several weeks of intensive
work ensued. The actual making of the slides was not what took
most of the time, although arranging with one of the fathers to
take the pictures required careful planning. Rather, the time went
into many serious discussions of what really were the funda-

mentals of democracy and in what manner their group had worked to put democratic principles to work. After they had singled out the points they wished to make and had decided what activities would illustrate them, they had the problem of writing captions for each picture.

Showing the series of slides did help parents gain an understanding of what was being attempted in that room. Probably even more educational than the slides themselves was the talking which the children did at home while the slides were being constructed. Undoubtedly the greatest strides in learning were made by the children. When the slides had been shown and this fifth grade group was ready to go on with other work, they were able to understand what was involved in locating a group need, and it was they who frequently said, "Let's stop to examine the way we are working."

In order that children may understand what they are doing as a legitimate kind of forward-looking school activity, the teacher may introduce some experience. For example, the teacher of a sixth grade showed her class two films, "Children Learning Through Experiences" and "Near Home." They compared what was said in the films with what they were doing in their own classroom. They listed the statements made in the "Children Learning Through Experiences" film and then analyzed "Near Home" to see if the principles set forth in the first film were put into practice. They checked this with what they were doing.

The teacher must continually help children develop their own standards and encourage them to use those standards as a basis for making choices and for determining the degree of success they have attained. By questioning children on why they are deciding as they are and why things have worked as they have, the teacher develops within them the ability and the desire to improve their own decisions and actions. After children begin to show an interest in evaluating progress, a teacher often suggests, when a group project is started, that the children give some thought to how they will know whether their plans are working. He helps them use their experience in other situations as a guide in planning new experiences. It is the function of the teacher to keep children examining the process used to achieve the results.

Children are likely to consider accomplishments only, until they have the importance of their way of working pointed out to them. When they see that it is through using group process that living is improved, the children themselves begin to do the major part of their evaluation in terms of finding ways of improving that process.

The teacher helps children recognize the individual growth they are achieving as they work together. He encourages them to examine the reasons for this growth. He makes it possible for community members to recognize the learnings which children are gaining. He helps make clear the power that they are gaining to work as effective citizens.

CHAPTER VI

Illustrations:
Helping Children Work Together

Teachers have many opportunities to help children learn to live and work together democratically. Through the attitudes they take toward children, teachers are laying a foundation for the kind of living that will take place in the classroom. In every classroom there should be some problems, projects, or areas of study that are receiving the attention of the whole group.

On the pages that follow are three examples of the kinds of problems, projects, or areas of study which have been undertaken by groups of children. All the teachers involved were attempting to help children learn the group process. Some teachers emphasized certain elements of the process more than others. Following each description there is a short analysis of the way the teacher helped the children gain an understanding of the process as the essence of democracy.

A First Grade Takes a Trip on the Ferry

The first graders of Perry School were playing in the park, where they went often, because the school yard was crowded and the park had such wonderful space. The group had spent several months together, during which they had felt free to express themselves. Hence, they were always on the alert for ideas which offered adventure, things they could do together.

They often watched the ferry cruise back and forth across the river. Miss Smith had found and read them a story about a ferryboat, which became one of their favorites. One day Susan wrote a poem about the boat and Miss Smith copied it on a page of the book in which their stories and poems were recorded.

One day Sammy said, "I'd like to ride on that old ferryboat." Then, with an enthralled look on his face he added, "Why doesn't our whole class go? That would make a swell trip."

Miss Smith waited to see how the other children would respond. Their "Let's! let's!" and "Could we?" showed that they were in complete agreement. Everyone sat down on the steps of the monument nearby. Miss Smith said, "We seem to be agreed that we would like to ride the ferry. Now we must see whether it is practical. What questions must we ask before we are ready to make a final decision?" Thus she was helping the children learn to consider the many aspects of a problem before arriving at a decision.

Some of the questions they asked were, "How much does it cost?" "Is it dangerous?" "Will the principal let us go?" "What would our folks think about it?" "Would we be able to walk to the ferry?" "Would we get back in time for lunch?" All of them important questions, too! As children gain experience in examining a problem they develop the ability to discover the most important areas of concern.

How could they get the answers? That would take some planning. To them planning was not new so they proceeded to organize for further investigation. John would ask his mother to call the ferry company and find out how much the ferry ride would cost. He announced that they must buy round-trip tickets. *Round-trip* was a new word to Sammy, so they stopped to discuss it. Miss Smith was alert to children's need to understand.

Ruth remarked that the ferry could not be dangerous or there would not be so many people riding on it. But perhaps it might be safe for grownups and not for children. Raymond would ask his father, who had traveled a great deal and would be certain to know. Why shouldn't every one of them ask his own parents what they thought? Sammy would ask the principal what he thought of the idea the very minute they got back to school. Frank's brother often went for a walk along the river so he would know how far it would be to the dock. *Dock* was another new word for some, so they paused a minute to note its meaning.

The next morning the children were still enthusiastic. Before school they told each other what their parents had said. When the bell rang they gathered eagerly for the usual sharing time and each child proudly gave his "report." The information included statements such as, "The ride costs five cents each way. It isn't dangerous." "Many children ride on it." "The principal thinks it would be a fine experience." "It is only six short blocks to the docks. We can walk." "The round trip takes only twenty minutes. We can easily be back for lunch." "Our parents say we can go."

Then came the problem of deciding what day. Many children wanted to go the very next day, but some thought they might need longer than that to get notes from all their parents. They began to argue. Rebecca had another idea. "I think," she said, "after that walk we might be hungry and we should take a picnic lunch to eat on the ferry." Wonderful! But that would take more time. "We'll put it off, then," they said, "a picnic and a ferryboat ride both in the same day would be swell. That's worth waiting for."

"How long will it take to do that much planning?" they wondered. Frank brought the calendar from Miss Smith's desk. Even at such an early age the children were learning to make use of resources. "Today is Wednesday," he said, "here it is, right here."

"Let's see," said Miss Smith. "What must we do to get ready for the picnic? That will make a difference in how much time we must allow." The children agreed that first they must decide on what they would take to eat. Sandwiches, of course, but what kind of sandwiches? Should they be peanut butter or jelly? Some one suggested, "Why not have both." Ruth thought they should frost some graham crackers as they had done last week for the party. Her suggestion was added to the list the teacher was putting on the board.

"We'll all be thirsty and need something to drink," Charles reminded them. What should that be? They could take milk or juice because the school cafeteria had both. Juice might be more refreshing, so the problem was easily decided.

"How do you propose to carry a big can of juice?" Miss Smith inquired. That was a real problem which had not occurred to them. Perhaps Miss Smith could carry it, but that did not seem right. Then John mentioned their red wagon. "Perfect," they said, "We'll put the juice and the sandwiches and the cookies in that and take it along."

Now for the time schedule. Tomorrow would be Thursday. On Friday they had assembly and on Mondays they were scheduled for an examination by the school doctor. The day would be Tuesday. The schedule was written on a big chart so that they could refer to it.

Tomorrow they would make out their shopping list—more planning to be done. On Monday they could go to the store before the doctor came. They appointed committees to do the work. A graham cracker committee was subdivided into mixing and spreading committees; then there were the peanut butter committee, the jelly committee, and the juice committee.

In preparing the sandwiches on Tuesday morning there was a mixup because no one had thought to plan for working space. All of them wanted to work on the little table in the doll corner at the same time. Miss Smith asked them to stop and think what they could do about space. With the help of some paper towels they soon made chairs into work tables.

By a quarter to ten, they were off, red wagon and all. The river was especially busy that morning. An excursion boat passed near them. Tugs were pulling huge barges. The juice committee had remembered paper cups but had forgotten a can opener, so one of the crew loaned them one when he saw their predicament. At the end of the ride, the captain came down to greet them and offered to take them on another round trip free of charge. Miss Smith helped them do some quick calculating of time and they answered yes.

As the children trudged up the hill back to school, they asked many questions which Miss Smith could not answer. They would ask their parents, too. Wednesday morning Mary brought in a story she had composed about a boat she had seen on the river.

The children were pleased with the trip and proud to have planned so well. Ann said, "If we always work things out that way we can be sure they will come out all right." "Yes," said Miss Smith, "a few of us could have done the job, but all of us together were able to do it better. Why is that?"

The children often commented later on what they had seen. Sometimes they brought in stories about boats and their paintings included many reminders of their very successful adventure.

This illustration shows one way in which a teacher helped some first graders work together. She felt that the children were able to arrive at sensible decisions if they were given the needed help in ways of making them. Taking a ferry ride might not have occurred to them if during the year they had not learned that all their ideas would be given careful consideration even though some of them could not be used. While the idea for the ride came from a suggestion made by one child, actually the background which brought forth the idea had been built over a period of time. The teacher had already taken the children exploring. They had commented on the things they saw and she had often introduced stories about them. The ferryboat had been the center of attention on many occasions. While the teacher was not building a specific background of experience designed to make the children want to take a ride on the ferry, she was building one from which many new interests would develop, one of which proved to be the ferry.

The teacher did not permit the decision to be made only on impulse. Even in first grade the children should not base their judgments merely on opinion. They did some research. No attempt was made, however, to insist that they make a study of boats. Their interest in boats showed in many of the things they did. Some time in the years ahead the interest begun here might lead them to further study. The learnings gained through planning and taking the excursion were sufficient to warrant the time and energy expended.

The children's understanding of the importance of arriving at decisions thoughtfully was evident in the way in which they arranged to investigate all sides of the problem. They showed evidences of a greater ability to plan together than that which is often expected of older groups.

A Fifth Grade Entertains Mothers at Tea

Early in the year the children had planned and given a program for their parents. Now someone suggested that they give a play for them. They liked to do plays. They had often put on dramatizations for the room across the hall, but Henry said he wanted them to do something grander before he invited his mother. Miss Reuben reminded them that it was only two days before Thanksgiving and that Christmas holidays were not far away. Several children said, "There's lots of time," and others were saying, "A play wouldn't be much work. It doesn't take long."

"Let's be realistic," said Miss Reuben, "We can do one if we wish, but we don't want to start anything we can't finish before the holidays. We'd want to do it well if our parents came." She suggested they list on the board the days they would have. Then they could make a sketchy plan that would help them see whether it could be done well in fifteen days. The play would have to be planned. Scenery and costumes would take time. Of course, they could dispense with scenery, but they did not want to. The auditorium would be hard to get, for so many classes wanted it just before Christmas. They would want a Christmas party and some room decorations. After a few minutes of sketchy planning everyone agreed that they could not give a play now.

Seena thought that perhaps they could do something else to entertain their mothers. Again the children were thoughtful. Sue thought a tea might be easier. Walter thought that if they decorated the room nicely their mothers could come to see the decorations. Miss Reuben suggested that they might sing some of their Christmas songs. The idea seemed good, but wouldn't that be as much work as a play? They would have to decorate their room, practice their songs, set the table, make the tea. But surely they could. Miss Reuben reminded them that getting a table arranged would require a bit of work. Again they worked out a time schedule. They decided that they would be able to do everything if they organized carefully.

Together they planned where they would place the table. They made over-all plans for the decoration of the room. They would have a Christmas tree and put under it the gifts they were making for their mothers. Then came another idea that they all liked— would it be possible to make winter corsages to pin on their mothers as they came in? That wouldn't be much work. Mrs. Jones, who had helped them with their flower arrangements in the fall, would surely come in and show them how to do it.

Miss Martin in the cafeteria would lend dishes. Someone must bring a tablecloth. Where would their mothers sit? The children had planned together on many other occasions so they were getting quite expert at it. They knew that their work could be done much more effectively if they took time to plan. Still, it took many periods.

Decorating the room would require careful organizing. If all of them planned the over-all scheme then small groups and individuals could plan the details. In that way they could save time. Several suggestions were made but no one showed much enthusiasm. Emily had a brainstorm. Why not center everything in one theme? That sounded good; what would she suggest? Wouldn't it be fun to pretend this was the inside of Santa's workshop? They could get ideas from the story Miss Reuben had read about the workshop. Children from the primary grades would enjoy seeing it, too.

They would make the hall door look like the outside of a house. The blackboards would have window panes drawn on them with outdoor scenes in colored chalk. They had many ideas but they did not seem to be able to organize them. Miss Reuben asked them if they could think of a better way to get the work done. They decided to divide into groups so that each group would work out a plan and present it to the larger group. When they began reporting they found that several of the ideas were similar; however, each plan had its own distinctive feature. They suggested several possible ways of using the ideas. Finally, they appointed the chairman of each committee to a central committee to work the distinctive features of each plan into an over-all plan. This new plan was presented to the group, and after many changes they were ready to organize for work.

A list of tasks was drawn up and each child chose to work on the one that appealed most to him. As the children were constantly running out of materials or thinking of something they could use from some other room, Miss Reuben felt that they should develop better work habits. They must remember that there were other people in the building. She outlined the difficulty and asked the children to work on it. They tried to find out what was causing the trouble. They had made over-all plans but because of the time limits they had proceeded rather impulsively. They now worked out a plan for checking supplies each evening. The teacher could have made some rules to solve the problem but much more effective results were achieved by including the children in the planning process. They were learning to think of those beyond their immediate group.

As soon as the children finished their particular parts of the work, they began to do other things. There were invitations to be printed and napkins to be decorated. Proper ways of serving and behaving at a tea were discussed and introductions were practiced. Duties for the afternoon were outlined by the group.

At the tea everyone seemed to have a good time, but afterwards the children realized that many things could have been improved. The water for the tea had not been put on soon enough. There was too much to do at the last minute. More careful planning would have forestalled such difficulties. But the class had accomplished a tremendous amount of work. It hardly seemed possible that they had done everything in three weeks. So much was accomplished because they were interested in what they were doing. The project had been highly important to them, so they had used the best ideas that everyone had to offer. They had helped one another and had been willing to abide by the decisions of the group.

It should be noted that the teacher did not permit the children to begin a project without carefully considering all of its implications. She did not keep them from doing the play and would even have permitted it had that been the final decision. She did, however, point out possible difficulties which they might not have foreseen. She did not dictate standards but she called their attention to the fact that they would want to set up some if they were going to give a play for their parents.

Much time was spent in evaluating the project because the teacher wanted the children to appreciate the ideas that came as a result of thinking together. She wanted them to verbalize the values which came from a division of responsibility within an over-all plan that everyone had helped make. Thus they analyzed how they had worked and they would profit from working that way again.

A Seventh Grade Organizes a Weather Bureau

The seventh grade had been working on a unit, "The Weather —What Makes It?" They had studied cloud formations and had done several experiments with air pressure, including making a barometer with mercury. The forecasting of weather fascinated them. They began to check weather forecasts and it seemed as if the weatherman was wrong much of the time. The children often brought tales of their fathers' having said that they could do a better job without any fancy instruments, but the children did not quite believe them.

Since Harry's uncle received weather maps every day, Joe and Harry became interested in doing their own forecasting. They would write on the blackboards and then turn on a portable radio to get the official weather bureau forecast. It was not many days until the other children were wanting to do it, too. Why did they not turn the room into a weather station and act as a bureau for the whole school?

There was no point in starting a weather bureau unless they could be reasonably successful. If forecasting the weather was so simple, why did the men at the weather bureau have to study so hard? They had taken many courses in meteorology. How could the children find out what their own chances of success were? Why not ask the weather forecasters themselves?

Inquiries brought the information that in the area there were four different stations where weather was carefully studied; two of them were official, one at the airport and the other downtown; two were private companies which had their own bureaus. The director of the bureau at the airport said he would be glad to answer their questions and show them the equipment and methods used.

This trip must be carefully planned. Making the arrangements for getting there proved easy but there would be a great deal to learn after they did get there. Much preliminary work would be needed in order to make the best use of the weatherman's time. There was first of all the central question: Will it be possible for us to achieve reasonable success in forecasting the weather? If the answer should be negative, they would just get as much general information as possible about the bureau. If the answer should be affirmative, then they would have to ask many specific questions.

The teacher helped them organize a list of questions. She suggested that there were gaps, points at which they really did not have enough information on which to base questions. A committee was organized to study each area where these gaps seemed to exist. Children volunteered to work in the areas which interested them most. After two days, the class spent ninety minutes listening to reports. They looked at their original outline of questions and added additional questions gained from the reports. In two cases they asked committees to do additional research, as there were resources the committees had not used.

The teacher showed them how to listen in order to gain the most from the reports. She suggested ways of organizing their notes, and she encouraged them to find other ways themselves. She asked them to keep their proposed project in mind as they listened to the reports so that they could ask probing questions. As a result the children unearthed more gaps in their own understanding.

Only three days before the trip and there was still some additional research to do, and they must spend some time in planning for the conference with the weatherman. There were dangers in over-planning it. If their own study were weighted too much in one direction or another, they would lose the opportunity to see their problems in a new perspective when they got to the weather station. On the other hand, the man might not recognize all of the problems of a seventh grade that wished to establish a weather bureau of its own.

They agreed to encourage him to tell them whatever he considered important at the beginning of the conference. As it went on, they would decide whether to press their own questions. If what he was saying was really giving them help in getting started, they would ignore their own list and ask questions spontaneously when his information became too sketchy. If, on the other hand, he was being too general, they would tell him they had a list of questions and ask him whether he would be willing to help with some of them.

The weatherman encouraged them to start their own bureau because he thought that they could be reasonably successful. Back at school discussion hinged on what equipment they should have and how to get it. They decided to confine themselves to the following:

> a barometer they would make themselves
> a barometer they would borrow from the high school science laboratory

three thermometers, to be placed about the school
a rain gauge they would construct
a wind vane
thermometers, which many homes had outside their windows
weather maps

The children found that they had the equipment for making a barometer. The school had two good thermometers, and one of the children would bring a third. There were directions for making a rain gauge in one of their science books, and Harry's uncle would allow them to use his maps. The barometer from the high school laboratory was the big problem. They were not all sure that the high school teacher would want them to have it. They spent much time in deciding how to arrange for it and it was finally decided that the principal would be asked to make the request.

What they would do with the forecasts once they were finished was another consideration. Children in other classes were very much interested and they would want to know what success the seventh grade was having. But what if they were not successful in their attempts? They feared they might become the target of many wisecracks. It was agreed, however, that they would not mind such joking when they all faced it together.

They reserved the front bulletin board. One caption said *Government Bureau Forecasts,* another said *Seventh Grade Bureau Forecasts,* with enough space below each so that the forecasts could be legibly written. Lower on the board were the captions *Yesterday's Forecasts: Government, Seventh Grade, The Weather.*

The first few days of forecasting were hard ones. The children found they didn't know as much as they thought they did. They tried to get as many people as possible to check their judgments, so fathers were commissioned to make some observations from downtown offices. One boy called his father at an appointed hour every day to get additional "info," as he called it.

The local librarian was besieged with requests for more detailed information. There were deep scientific discussions. Old words took on new significance. When it was found that other children often misunderstood what they meant, they began analyzing each word before a report was issued. They tried to make their paragraphs clear and concise. All of this required much discipline in writing.

When they found that the government bureau was "hitting it" much more often than they, they kept a record in percentages. One morning they posted a huge bulletin, which read:

The weatherman is right 88 per cent of the time. We are right 67 per cent of the time. This happens because:

Our equipment is faulty.

Weather maps get here too late.

We do not know enough about the behavior of air pressure.

The community had heard a great deal about their study because mothers and fathers had been in on making the forecasts. Many fathers stopped making rash statements about how much better they were than the weatherman, but the children felt that there were still many faulty concepts. They decided to have a series of meetings to help answer people's questions and give pertinent weather information. There would be an evening meeting for fathers and mothers and one meeting for children in the afternoon.

Before deciding which classes to invite, the children asked the teachers which children were interested and could understand it. Different groups would understand different kinds of information. Instead of one afternoon meeting, they found they needed to hold three.

In their evaluation of the project, the children recognized that they had acquired much specialized information on weather and had broadened their interest and knowledge in many related areas. They saw even better than before the importance of organizing their thinking and were developing in their ability to do it.

They recognized that the idea had developed from the interest of a small group. The whole group, however, was already engaged in a study of weather at a more theoretical level. The small group had called their attention to a practical way of continuing their study. The teacher gave the children help in gaining new skills as they felt a need for them. She had to give them some very definite preparation before they visited the weather bureau.

CHAPTER VII

Illustrations: Helping Children Organize School Services

Every school has many services that help make the school run smoothly. The book room is set up to dispense books to the children; the art supplies are arranged so that they can be delivered with the least possible effort. These school services are organized and managed by the principal and teachers. Thus the children miss one of the most valuable experiences the school can provide. These projects are important to the work going on in the whole building. Why, then, should teachers do the ordering of books and the distributing of them after they arrive? Why should an art supervisor spend weeks working alone on an art inventory and requisition list? Why should cafeteria workers have the full responsibility for the arrangement of the cafeteria? Why should one teacher struggle with ordering all the audio-visual materials?

These and many other activities provide means by which children can learn to work together to improve the quality of living in the entire school. The four illustrations in this chapter describe how teachers and children have worked together and, in so doing, have learned much about group process.

A Fifth Grade Orders Art Supplies

In Columbus School the children were responsible for ordering and distributing the art supplies. They began their work while they were still fifth graders and continued with it in the sixth grade.

They began planning soon after Christmas. After formulating a set of plans, they analyzed its advantages and disadvantages and worked on it to make it better. When they had a plan of action that seemed workable, they discussed it with the principal and district art supervisor, whose suggestions became the basis for revisions.

Then they organized for work. Many children wrote to art supply companies for catalogs. A committee met with the art supervisor to make a list of the kinds of supplies and equipment already in use. From this they made an inventory form on which teachers could note the quantity of each item they had on hand and the amount they thought would be required in the next year. The children wrote a letter to accompany the requisition forms. The children themselves set up the criteria for the letter. They tried to make it clear, courteous, and brief.

The art supervisor brought some new media to their room and the children tried them out to see whether they should be ordered. They liked them but decided to have a small group of first graders and third graders try them out, too. What appealed to a fifth grade might not be suitable for first grade.

Paper came in many weights. When was it economical to buy the cheapest weight? For what purposes was a more expensive weight needed? In deciding, they found it necessary to try the kinds of paper with each medium. Brushes were all sizes and qualities. Large paint brushes cost a dollar each. The children decided that they would henceforth think twice before mistreating them.

After selecting the items they thought were best suited for the purpose intended, they decided to consult the teachers. What would be the most effective method? They decided to explain the plan at a faculty meeting. Then the class divided into committees and each committee conferred with two teachers.

Tabulating the results and writing orders for the central office was an ardous task. It was easy to make errors in adding and multiplying when counting the total of each item and figuring the costs. On some items the district would get a discount. That also had to be figured. When the blanks were filled in, the children checked and rechecked.

They selected a committee to go with the principal and art supervisor to the office of the Superintendent of Schools. He looked at the total figure and groaned. Then he smiled at the children and said, "That's more than we have to spend. I wonder where we can cut." The children asked pertinent questions about the budget. How had he decided how much could be spent? They would need this information when they reported to their larger group. They knew something about taxes and had heard their fathers complain about them, but they had not realized that taxes had anything to do with the supplies used at school. The superintendent looked again at their detailed list and made several suggestions. They agreed to go back to school and see what they could do.

Again, they did much planning. With whom should they confer? They decided to give the information to teachers or to entire classes, depending upon who had met with them before. They drafted a letter explaining the situation. Some teachers who had previously done all of the deciding themselves asked that the children in their classes be included. Fathers and mothers also became interested. There were many suggestions and they were able to cut the total order.

Then a plan was made whereby supplies needed first could be ordered first and delivered before school started in the fall. Plans for storing and taking care of the materials for the rest of the year were postponed until September at which time the amount of space available would be known.

In the fall two storerooms were piled high with the supplies that had arrived during the summer. One committee worked several days locating and delivering them. When school started the children attempted to organize them. The janitor would have to put the heavy packages of paper on the shelves, and it was important that the space to be occupied by such things be planned in advance. A group of six took the responsibility for doing this.

A system was organized whereby teachers' requisitions could be filled quickly and correctly. Every week the class evaluated what had been done and arranged to straighten out any problems that had arisen. On some occasions special requisitions for supplies for which the group had not foreseen a need had to be sent to the Superintendent.

Through taking an active part in the ordering of their supplies, the children learned to make plans and test them in action, as well as to carry through responsibilities. A part of the school program depended on their efforts. The results of their work would be genuinely important to them and to other children in the school. The teacher played an important part throughout the project. He was constantly helping them evaluate progress. Since adjustments in plans had to be made as emergencies arose, the whole program had to be flexible.

A Fourth Grade Organizes a Lost and Found Department

This rough and tumble group consisted of nine girls and twenty-four boys. They climbed over fences, rolled in the leaves, snatched each other's hats, and were in general a tempestuous crew. Wherever they went they lost things. Galoshes, gloves, gym shoes, sweaters, caps were always being searched for, and someone was almost always on his hands and knees looking through the articles in the little nook where such things had been thrown when found. Their teacher never had a dull moment.

George came in snorting, "What this school needs is some organization. That lost and found place is a mess. I don't know why the janitor doesn't clean it up once in a while." "How could he?" the others wanted to know. "People are always throwing things there."

After that, almost everyone who went to hunt something returned to complain. Tired of such constant criticisms meant for no one in particular, Alice asked them why they didn't do something about it if they found it so disagreeable. "Why don't we do something?" Michael countered, "What can we do?"

We could agree to keep it cleaned up and in order," she retorted.

"That wouldn't do any good," some of the boys replied, "because kids would come in and tear things up as soon as we got them fixed."

Miss Ruth asked whether there were not some way of avoiding this. At first the children could not think of any. After all, people did have to go in to hunt their things. Jenny thought that perhaps the boy patrols should take charge of it. Then Frank had an idea. Why didn't they take care of it themselves? The group was rather stunned by this suggestion. Robert did not see what good that would do. The big boys wouldn't pay any attention to them. Besides, no matter how many times the nook was straightened out, the children would get it out of order as soon as no one was on duty. After all, they couldn't stay there every minute.

Miss Ruth began to list the problems on the board:

> Older boys might not pay any attention to fourth graders.
> There is no way of keeping it in order.
> The fourth grade can't have someone on duty all the time.

She asked if there were any ways of meeting these difficulties? Susan thought that there was no way as long as the lost and found was in that particular corner where things could not be locked up. She thought that if an adequate place was provided, the other problems could be managed. The children wanted to run to Mr. Jones immediately to see if he knew of any other place that could be used.

Miss Ruth asked whether they were really interested in doing the work that would be required to put and keep a place in order. There was no point in asking Mr. Jones until they had found out how many children were interested. She suggested that it might be wise to think about it for a while. Perhaps the next day they could consider some of the problems that they might encounter.

The next day there was still enthusiasm for the lost and found project. It would be fun to do and besides it would be a service to the school. They ought to do something for the school sometimes. Some were hesitant. What kind of work would be involved? Would it be possible to do it well? Would they be able to get the equipment they needed?

They discussed the way a lost and found center should operate. There were some differences of opinion but these were easily dissolved. The idea sounded better and better as they talked. More children became interested. They made a list of the equipment they would need and some of the kinds of work involved as follows:

> Shelves for small items
> Hangers for coats and jackets
> A table to be used as a counter
> A system for recording articles lost and found
> Someone on duty at certain hours

There would be much work but when it was listed that way it did not seem impossible.

Now they could check to see whether Mr. Jones would approve of such a plan. If so, could he suggest a locked room? "Let's send someone down to ask him right now," seemed to be the general opinion. "Have you thought about what you will say?" asked Miss Ruth. "We have been disgusted with the lost and found arrangements for a long time. We have been discussing the problem directly for two days. To us it is very clear, but probably Mr. Jones has not lost anything, and if we came racing in, he may be confused."

A committee was appointed to visit Mr. Jones. Before they went, they were to line up their points and plan how they would present their proposal. During the next day's planning period the other children would check their plans.

Mr. Jones suggested that they use the large supply closet down the hall from their room. The supplies there could easily be put somewhere else. That would make it convenient for Miss Ruth to supervise and easier for the children to carry out their assignments.

They went on a tour of investigation. Two of the boys took the measurements. The room would need much cleaning. Mr. Jones did not feel that they could afford to paint it and he did not want them to paint it themselves. There were already shelves, but there were no hangers.

Back in their own classroom the children began to plan. The problem had several parts. They must find a way to get hangers. They must work out a filing system for checking things in and out. They must arrange for the hours when the room would be open and for who would be on duty.

They attacked the problem of getting hangers first. They would speak to the custodian. Were there any frames with hangers on them in the building? Did he know of anything that could be used as a substitute? Could hangers be made?

At the end of a long planning session, committees to undertake the following assignments were organized:

> Confer with the custodian.
>
> Interview three teachers to get their ideas concerning the times of day when the center could best be open.
>
> Work out a system for receiving and returning objects.

Work out a list of regulations to be posted in all the classrooms.

Plan a sign to be placed above the door.

Help the custodian get the room cleaned.

The work of each committee was considered by the whole class. Suggestions were made on ways to organize for work. Committees were not to go hastily to the custodian or to teachers for interviews. They must think carefully about what they wanted to find out and then plan the kind of approach and questions that would help them to get as much information as possible. Good ideas presented for the consideration of the other committees were presented also.

The next three days were busy ones. When a committee had completed its assignment, it gave a report to the rest of the class. Sometimes the reports were accepted without much question. Sometimes much discussion followed and changes were made. For example, the committee that was considering ways of informing the rest of the school of the procedures to be followed had worked out an announcement to be given in assembly. Class members felt that this might be good for the upper grades but that the first grade and kindergarten would not understand. They finally decided they would not try to tell the youngest ones about the change. Rather they would give each one very careful attention when he lost something.

Almost every report outlined more work. The entry and release system would require the hectographing of some forms. The regulations must be hectographed, too. The custodian would construct a frame for hangers but the children must requisition the materials he would need.

Groups were reorganized to do the work outlined. Every day each group gave a very short report of its progress. Finally a working schedule was set up, arranged so that no one would be out of the room too often or too long.

What must they know in order to work in the center? They reviewed the regulations. They practiced filling out the forms. They discussed the importance of being polite even when others were not. They outlined what they would do if children who came to the center were disorderly. Six at a time they went down to the center and Susan and Joe showed them just where the forms were kept. Ray explained how items were to be numbered.

The center was open from nine until nine-thirty each morning and from two-thirty until three each afternoon. By the second morning unforseen difficulties had arisen. There was no one to receive items that had been found during noon hour. The afternoon period was changed to one o'clock. It was evident that some children would be asking twice a day about their lost articles unless something were done to prevent them. This problem took much discussion and could not be settled in one day. Eventually they solved it by means of a form which a child filled out if his lost articles had not been found. He gave his room number so that he could be notified if they were returned.

There were times when the children in charge preferred to be in the classroom and would have liked to neglect their responsibilities. When they were all going on an excursion or when something unexpected happened, a notice was sent to all the rooms stating that the center would be closed. On the whole, it operated smoothly.

The evaluation made by the children at the end of the year revealed some of their reasons for feeling that the project had been successful:

> Everyone was behind it.
> We didn't jump into it without thinking what we were doing.
> We consulted the principal and other people who could give us ideas.
> We didn't take the first plans that occurred to us.
> We paid attention to the ideas of everyone.
> We kept checking to see how things were going. If we were not satisfied we tried to find out what was wrong. Then we found ways of correcting it.
> We were willing to change our plans when they didn't seem to work well.

The teacher, in this instance, helped children develop a way of meeting their own needs and at the same time of helping others meet theirs. She recognized that on so long-range a venture it was important that special care be taken in making the decision. Even though they did not see all the implications, they could be helped to locate them by investigation. The teacher was alert to the techniques of the work the children would need to do the job. She worked closely with them to help them develop a way of approaching the principal.

The committees did wonderful work. Their careful planning resulted in a dove-tailing of activities. The teacher wanted to make certain that the children recognized that the organization was effective and that they knew why. Here was an opportunity to evaluate with them all the aspects of the process they had used.

A Fifth Grade Shares in the May Festival

The May festival, which the P.T.A. held every year as a means of raising funds, was just a month away. It had become such a tradition that the whole neighborhood looked forward to this festival. This year the intermediate and upper grade rooms were being invited to share in it. There were to be eight booths for games of skill.

The fifth grade was delighted at the invitation. They were willing to do any work it might entail and to work very hard to finish the projects already under way in order to allow time for this very intriguing new one.

Miss Spencer discussed the nature of the games. What was meant by games of skill? They discussed the qualities which games should have in order to be a popular attraction. The children had many at the tips of their tongues, but they decided not to depend merely on their own judgment. They might decide on a game that would appeal only to the fifth grade. Who would the customers be? They would ask their younger brothers and sisters what made a game fun for them. They would ask their mothers and fathers. From time to time they made suggestions, which Miss Spencer wrote on a blackboard at the side of the room. Finally the following criteria were set up:

The game must
—be difficult enough to make people want to play.
—not be so difficult that most people could not do it.
—provide some easier goal for the younger children.
—be different from those ordinarily seen at carnivals.
—be safe.
—be played quickly so that the waiting line would not be too long.

What could they find that would fulfill all these requirements? Some of the suggestions for games were immediately ruled out as not meeting all the criteria. They finally narrowed the list down to four, and decided to put together some impromptu equipment and experiment a bit to see how practical the ideas were. The decision was eventually made in favor of a ring-toss game. The target was to be the nose of a huge clown which they would construct from papier-mache.

While plans were in progress, everything suddenly came to a standstill. The children learned that the seventh grade was planning something similar. Some of the children began to grumble about stealing ideas, but they came to see that groups could very easily have similar ideas. No one was to blame, but something must be done.

Planning for the game itself was at a standstill but here was a bigger challenge. How could this duplication be eliminated? The children suggested sending a note to the seventh grade asking them to select a different kind of game. But why should the seventh grade change its plans? Why not the fifth grade? How could this problem be solved? It would be foolish for them to proceed if the seventh grade also continued.

Why not meet with the seventh grade? Where would they meet? Who would act as chairman? What kinds of questions should be asked? How? What a lot of plans to be made! They needed to learn more about conducting meetings, too. All of this had to be done quickly as the time before the festival was very short.

The meeting was a good one. The fifth graders conducted themselves in a far more sensible manner than their original reactions indicated. Their conduct was especially praiseworthy in view of the fact that the results were not what they had hoped. The seventh graders had done their planning two days before they had and the plans they had made were even more exciting than any the fifth graders had imagined. The clown at whom the rings were to be tossed was to be alive and would do a trick each time his artificial nose was circled.

The fifth graders were proud of the meeting. They had learned a great deal about parliamentary procedures and the importance of discussing disagreements. They recognized the importance of looking at other people's motives and intentions as well as their own.

They were ready to begin again but they discovered something else. It was not necessary to begin again. They could have chosen one of the three remaining ideas on their original list. After all, it had taken two days to choose one of them. Instead of using the old list, however, they thought of new ideas, better ideas than they had had in the first place. Out of their deliberations came a fantastic marble game which made use of a maze of tunnels. It was different from anything they had ever seen.

"Why is it that we have better ideas now?" Miss Spencer asked. Why was it that they had not thought of these latest ones in the beginning. It would have saved time. That was a hard one. "Why was it?" the children wondered. From time to time they speculated about it. Eventually many of them saw that the later suggestions came as a result of the thinking that had gone into the initial suggestions. Each new experience multiplied their ideas. They also noted that the time was not wasted. Think how much they learned. Learning came out of the way they worked as well as from what they studied.

Children at this age want very much to be in the center of activity. They like to be included in what the upper grades are doing. The teacher took this opportunity to help them learn ways of fitting into a whole situation. The learning they received in working through a problem with an older group of children was very valuable.

A Sixth Grade Gives Projector Service

Richard and Alvin had helped Miss Stevens as she set up the sound projector. They tarried after school to help put it away. Richard could not contain his desires. "I wish I could learn to run that thing," he said. "I think I could do it." Miss Stevens thought a moment. Why shouldn't he learn? She showed him how to thread the machine and the next week he did it again with only a little help. Alvin wanted to learn, too. He succeeded but it took him a little longer to do it alone.

As they threaded the machine the boys asked questions. What makes the sound? What would happen if we didn't put it around this knob? Miss Stevens told them frankly that she did not know. They began reading the manual to find out.

Could the boys operate the machine when the film was shown Wednesday? Miss Stevens knew that some of the other children would want to learn how when they saw that Richard and Alvin knew. Why shouldn't they? She could help any who really wanted to learn. Yes, the boys could operate the machine but she would check to be certain that everything was in order before they turned on the electricity.

The children were surprised when Alvin and Richard set up the projector without any help. Although a few were fearful and did not want to try, Miss Stevens set aside several noon hours and some time after school for those who wished to learn.

Richard had gone to the library and had two books to show the class. With the aid of a simple sketch which he drew on the board he demonstrated what conveyed the sound. There was material about the lens, too, but he had not had time to study it.

The children found operating the projector fascinating. It was too bad, though, that they did not have more films to show so that they could get the experience more often. Miss Stevens had an idea but she would check it before mentioning it to the children. She asked some of the teachers if they would be willing to have the sixth graders operate the machine for them.

Next she consulted the principal. He was dubious, as she had known he would be. Those machines were expensive. What if something should happen to them? She reminded him that the machine got out of repair even when teachers operated it, for some teachers were quite careless with it. He knew this was true. As she had always handled equipment carefully, he agreed to let her try her scheme.

The sixth graders were delighted. At first they could not believe their luck. Of course, they would organize such a service. They would willingly undergo any inconveniences or hard work that it would entail. Even those who did not care to operate equipment were enthusiastic. They wanted to include an additional service. They would take care of ordering all audio-visual materials and would be responsible for checking them in and out of the building. These sixth graders welcomed not only the opportunity to operate the projectors, but even more the chance to play responsible roles in the building. They liked the idea of going into other rooms to perform important services.

They agreed that many of them did not yet have the skill to do the job. Those who had it would be the ones to go first. Someone who was still learning would go along to assist. They wrote on the board "We are not to rush!" because they felt that damages were most likely to occur to machine or film if they hurried.

Miss Stevens felt that the little knowledge they had was not enough. She wanted someone who really understood the equipment to give them careful instruction. The principal was an expert. He agreed to take the children who had mastered the technique of setting up the equipment four at a time and instruct them in every detail, explaining the reasons for everything and preparing them to deal with any emergencies.

The children planned that one period each morning should be given to ironing out difficulties. The committee responsible for ordering materials would meet twice a week. In that way they would not divert too much time from other projects which they had under way. Blanks on which requests for services were to be made were prepared and distributed to every room. On receipt of these forms, a confirmation of the time and hour was then sent to the teachers.

The service was initiated and the children found it was fun. They not only gained a feeling of importance but had opportunity to see many films. Often they would return to the classroom with the news that the film they had just shown would be helpful to the sixth grade. If they could give reasonable evidence that the film would really give them needed help, they were allowed to show it. They developed the ability to evaluate materials and established a card index which gave a description of the film, who had seen it, what groups might profit from it.

Before long Miss Stevens realized that this particular project was taking a great deal of time. While it was a valuable experience, she felt that they should be free to enjoy other experiences, too. The actual service given in other classrooms did not take more time than had been expected, but organizing to take care of the services was steadily encroaching on other phases of the program. Class work was interrupted constantly by requests.

She frankly told the group that they would have to consider giving up the project unless they could operate with greater efficiency. Miss Stevens felt that they could do something about it and also that it was important for them to learn to organize more efficiently. The discussion that followed revealed the potential the children had for improving their organization. Miss Stevens suggested that first they analyze the way they had been working to see if they could define any specific difficulties. They had been so busy making arrangements that they had not bothered to evaluate their ways of working. It took a while for them even to think in terms of the whole classroom situation.

What were the difficulties? Teachers were sending their requests at different times. There were always problems to discuss, and they took time. Everything seemed to be someone else's fault. Could plans be laid in such a way that these difficulties could be removed? Did teachers' requests have to come to the room? Could there be a box in the office from which they would be picked up once a day? Could all problems be channeled into the morning period which had been set aside for such discussion?

In order to shorten their proceedings they would have to delegate responsibilities to smaller groups. They had been giving the same amount of attention to all problems. Were there some problems to which they should give a great deal of attention and others which, once a policy had been established, an individual or a group could take care of?

Sometimes the children would forget the decision to keep group discussion to policy making. A committee was formed to evaluate items of business. They talked to those who presented problems about ways of solving them without taking group time. The children were amazed at how effectively the services operated. It was much better than it had been before. Miss Stevens emphasized the importance of having everyone included in policy-making decisions. She pointed out that the policies are valuable only if people made use of them. The group learned that some decisions are made by a total group, some by small groups, and others by individuals.

The teacher insisted that when the children had agreed to fit into a situation they carry out their responsibilities. She herself analyzed their ways of working. She helped them experiment with many ways of working together. They were then able to develop insight through comparing approaches and locating the principles which underlay each approach.

In the three examples cited, the teachers served as guides in helping children work effectively together. Through helping them evaluate their planning and action, they stimulated the children to improve their ways of working together.

CHAPTER VIII

The Teacher's Development

Much has been written to help teachers improve their ways of working, although much of the literature has treated the teacher as if he were separated from the world in which he lives. However, through teaching group process, he can become a more effective teacher and a more integrated member of his community.

The Teacher's Study and Planning

It is often assumed that teachers who are attempting to work democratically in their classrooms need make no preparation outside of class. Some teachers take it for granted that to do so would be to admit that they are attempting to thrust a predetermined curriculum upon the children. After all, they say, the needs are to be defined by the children. Children and teacher do the planning and the evaluation. What can there be for the teacher to do?

Such a point of view ignores the fact that the democratic process is learned. Children do not come to school already experts in its use. Even if they came to school already knowing how to work together democratically the teacher still must do much planning and make much preparation.

Unless a teacher does make a great deal of preparation, he will not be able to give children the quality of help they should have. Every phase of working cooperatively requires careful pre-planning by the teacher. We do not mean to imply that he will plan what the children will do within the process. That is a function of the process itself. The teacher brings to the situation knowledge which will help the children to use the process more effectively. The teacher's preparation will be largely in the areas of familiarizing himself with the characteristics of the children as individuals and as group members, finding out what the present interests of the children are and what kinds of interests they are likely to develop in the future, building a background knowledge of the content and resources which might be helpful in a pursuit of those interests, studying the community, and studying the dynamics of the group in order to give help in improving the quality of the process.

STUDYING CHILDREN'S BACKGROUND

A teacher can learn much through a study of his children. How do they feel about themselves, their peers, their parents, their community? From what kinds of backgrounds do they come? What is the source of family income? Are both parents employed? Who are the children's friends? What kinds of relationships do they have with these friends? What do they do during their vacations?

The teacher learns the children's backgrounds in a number of ways. He observes them. What are their attitudes when they arrive in the morning? Do they look as if someone had helped them get ready for school? Do they have much to share? Do they play with the other children? Are there cliques or gangs within the group? Are they able to organize group games readily?

What characteristics are common to children of this age group? In what ways do the children reveal these characteristics? Does the group seem more or less mature than other children of this age level?

The teacher examines the records on each child. Do the health reports indicate that certain individuals will need special consideration. Are there wide differences in ability? In what areas have the children shown special abilities? Is there any record of special talents which have been developed by individual members of the group?

The childrens' former teachers can give much personal information which may reveal some of their difficulties. This information may also indicate the feelings these teachers had toward the children and how the children may feel toward adults.

STUDYING CHILDREN'S INTERESTS

A study of the neighborhood in which they live will give much helpful information on what children's needs are likely to be. The teacher observes the psychological climate of the community. How do people behave toward each other? What are their major interests? How do they satisfy these interests?

The teacher watches the children's reactions to many kinds of school tasks. He notes the questions they ask, the comments they make during class discussion and play time. What materials in the classroom especially arouse their interests? What do they choose to read?

What do the children do outside of school hours? How do they feel about community happenings? World news? What do they consider to be the high spots in their lives? In school, what direction have their efforts taken in the past? In which areas did they express the most enthusiasm? In which of the arts have they had an opportunity to explore? The teacher observes the kinds of things the children write and paint. When they have adequate time and materials with which to work they will reveal many of their hopes and fears through creative expression.

A survey of the kinds of activities which similar classes have found helpful may offer some insight into possibilities for this group. No two groups will express needs in exactly the same way, but there will be many areas of common concern which may provide a reference point the teacher can use in arranging a stimulating and satisfying environment.

It may be helpful for him to list needs he thinks the children might have, recognizing that many significant ones may escape his attention. One list might be of specific emotional and physical needs which appear be pressing. One sixth grade teacher, for instance, noted that his group seemed to have special need for improved working relationships with other classes in the building, a need to develop respect for their own creative abilities, and a need to develop better physical coordination. On another list he included ways in which he thought the children might express their needs. He noted such things as the need for a baseball field and the need for a place to play on rainy days.

STUDYING THE COMMUNITY

The teacher's study of the environment enables him to make effective use of it. He learns about the children and about their possible areas of interest. A study of the immediate community will reveal many resources. What facilities does it have for children? What facilities are needed? What industries are located in the area? What kinds of buildings are being constructed? Searching for the answers to these questions will reveal many potential experiences and materials for use by the children.

The teacher also studies the community to see what problems people face. To what extent are they aware of these problems? What are they doing about them? What are the implications of their actions or failure to act? How will all of this affect children? To what extent are children likely to feel a personal interest? How can these problems be called to their attention? What would a study of them involve? In what kinds of action could children engage? How could they work with the adults to improve the community? How can they be made cognizant of the larger forces which bring about such needs for improvement?

The teacher searches for ways in which he can help children broaden the base of their activity. Cooperative work encourages realistic venturing into fundamental issues. Children delight in being active participants in a community if someone will help them locate the ways in which they can make meaningful contributions.

There are two very different points of view concerning how children broaden their concepts of community and develop their own feelings of responsibility as community members. Some teachers present children with adult problems and help them perform as miniature adults in working out these problems. Other teachers begin with the needs that children themselves feel and help them to work with others. The children are guided to evaluate these interactions. They are encouraged to examine the existing relationships and the reasons for them. As the children's awareness is thus broadened, they become more and more active in community affairs. Always they work on those problems which are of special significance to them at their level of maturity.

Teachers who conscientiously follow either approach must be well-informed concerning the needs of the local community. If they accept the latter view, the use of group process, they must recognize not only the problems as seen by adults but also the relationship of children to the community, so that they can help them make significant improvements in their environment.

BUILDING SUBJECT MATTER BACKGROUND

The subject matter drawn upon depends on the expanding interests of the learners. This is the kind of subject matter that cannot be determined in advance. The teacher must learn to use written materials and his knowledge of human relationships in helping children utilize the appropriate subject matter for meeting their needs.

He must continually search for new knowledge that will help him develop a better understanding of people's needs and means for meeting them. In doing this, he will read many books, both those written for adults and those written for children. He will examine textbooks and magazines of all descriptions. He will not, however, furnish the subject matter children will use. Choice of subject matter will be made by teacher and children cooperatively. This function is an integral part of the total process.

Qualifications of the Teacher

As outlined in the preceding chapters, the role of the teacher is to help children understand and use the group process. The process is dynamic. Hence, a teacher must be very flexible. For every teacher to try to acquire the same characteristics denies the importance of diversity for democratic living. Those who use rigid standards in appraising teachers are using static techniques in an attempt to meet dynamic needs. Suppose we were to say, for example, that every teacher must know his community, or that he must be calm in the face of any emergency, or that he must get along well with people. It is true that all these are important attributes but we need not insist that every teacher have them all before he attempts to guide group process. A person who has not taken much interest in the community will become better and better acquainted with it as he works with children. He learns to know it in a practical way, and his new interest in it is sincere and sustained. A teacher who loses his temper in the face of frustrating circumstances may work well at other times and eventually develop self-control. Another teacher may not get along well with his peers, but as he helps children with their problems he will develop a new perception of himself in relation to his fellow teachers and may make continued improvement. There is no one type of teacher who is best fitted to help children work cooperatively, for children gain much from working with people of widely varying backgrounds.

Even though the qualifications of teachers cannot be set up as traits or combinations of traits it cannot be said that everyone has a personality suitable for teaching or that all teachers are equally able to learn the group process. Those who teach by means of group process must have dynamic qualifications. We must be concerned with the direction in which a teacher is moving as well as with the stage of development he has reached.

When a person is developing in a particular direction, he gains momentum which accelerates his movement in that direction. Guidance from others will focus the direction more clearly and increase the speed. The difficulty lies in changing the direction.

Because changing from one direction to another requires much time and effort, those who are moving in the direction of greater rigidity, greater dogmatism, and a more inflexible approach to problems cannot be expected to teach children a dynamic process without extensive change in personality. Many teachers who worked out a forward-looking, up-to-the-minute approach to teaching ten years ago are still using the same techniques. Because they had adopted the latest methods, they appeared to be flexible. A close examination at that time of the direction in which they were moving undoubtedly would have shown that they were thinking of people in a static way and were likely to become more and more rigid in their procedures.

Teachers who espouse liberal political causes may or may not be forward-looking in educational practice. At first thought it seems impossible that anyone who is liberal politically may not be liberal in other areas. But all those who support liberal causes may not necessarily be flexible in their thinking. Those who have reached a political stand thoughtfully are likely to work thoughtfully on educational problems. Those, however, who cling to liberal ideas because they feel it is the thing to do, because they want to be out in front, are by their manner indicating that they are moving toward rigidity.

Qualifications, then, must be stated as the potential for growth in process. Movement may be expressed through a desire to be more human, to work more freely with children, and to work more closely with others. We speak of growth rather than of a complete knowledge of process to emphasize that no one ever knows all there is to know about using it. As understanding of it develops, it is used more and more frequently in making decisions and in meeting highly important needs. As group process is used, ability to work with people and the desire to share ideas with them becomes stronger.

share idea

Change for change's sake may work against the best interests of the children. Teachers who move about aimlessly, attempting to be flexible, may eventually pull back into rigidity. A tiny bit of creative energy properly channelled can often accomplish a great deal more than much that is misdirected.

Movement in the direction we have described entails continuous growth on the part of the individual. This growth should be in two areas—his own personality must become more flexible, and his techniques for working in group situations must be improved. A teacher's attempt to change educational points of view and practices without at the same time making significant changes in his personality puts a great strain on him. It is almost certain to result in mechanical and spiritless school practices. A teacher should not change his way of working unless he himself feels an honest need for change. Some teachers experiment with group techniques only because they think they should. Because they have energy and drive they discover what to do and then organize to do it. Because they have no basic understanding of what they are doing, the whole procedure becomes machine-like. Mechanics which might otherwise be sensible become extraneous and fail to accomplish what they were originally designed to.

The development of a flexible personality and techniques for working with groups are dependent on each other. No series of steps can be prescribed for developing either. Personality is augmented in a dynamic situation as one uses the group process. Techniques are discovered as one works to improve the group situation. Personality, techniques, process—all are dynamic and interactive. If the development of any one is held back, all are stunted.

Reading about group process or discussing it with others will not necessarily ensure the incorporation of it as a way of working with children. Behavior is not changed merely through reading or discussion. The teacher must experience the use of the cooperative process as a satisfying way of meeting his own needs. As he uses it, change takes place within himself and he develops positive attitudes toward it which cause him to want to use it in many situations.

Developmental Activities

Although we have stated that there is no one course of action which will equip a teacher to work in this manner, there are several activities which may help a teacher in his development. Some are deeply significant, others are valuable only if one has an opportunity to work in group situations. Experimentation in process and enriched living should go on at the same time. Although a variety of experience will doubtless make a teacher a more understanding and interesting person, it cannot be taken for granted that if a teacher broadens his activities classroom practice will automatically become more democratic.

A discussion of some of the methods that may encourage teachers to use group process follows.

Analysis of an individual's experiences with cooperative group process. A backward look at groups which have accomplished things cooperatively gives an opportunity to look at the strength of process, at the way it works, and at its effect. Somewhere in his background almost everyone has one experience or more where a group cooperating accomplished a great deal. Everyone has had also the experiences where time was wasted and not much was accomplished. A careful study of both the successful and of the unsuccessful experiences can develop insight into the ongoing, interactive forces at work.

Through studying the reasons for the unusual success of some projects carried on in his own classroom, the teacher may locate certain trends. He may examine them to see the relationship between the children's needs and the work done. He may see what his own unique contribution was and strive to strengthen it in the future. A careful analysis of day-by-day experiences at school to find ways of making better use of the process will help deepen insights. Time taken to think through what is being done, to test it against one's philosophy of life and education, will help refine meanings and integrate learnings.

Working with groups of people who are concerned with refining their use of the process. There are professional groups whose primary concern is in this area. Attending their meetings gives opportunity to see what others consider to be forward-looking approaches, as well as a chance to share progress with individual teachers who have similar interests. Sometimes these organizations set up study groups in which group process techniques are either studied or tried out. Through these, people become familiar with the many different concepts of such terms as teacher-pupil planning, group dynamics, sociometric techniques, and social interaction.

Education courses in this field offer opportunities to meet others working for similar goals. Other teachers in the system or in adjoining systems make good resource persons. Sometimes classroom visits can be interchanged. Seeing what goes on somewhere else makes analysis on a broader basis possible.

Watching a professional group leader who has confidence in himself and his group is often especially helpful since it is hard for a teacher who has always had children glued in their seats to visualize order being achieved in any other arrangement. Community groups sometimes work together very well. They may present an opportunity to work cooperatively with one's peers in meeting community needs and so to get additional insight through experience at that level.

Widening acquaintance with a variety of people. It is inspiring to be around people who do things in a creative way. Those who feel secure enough to develop a positive approach to life help stabilize one's own relationship to a group. People of other professions often have background and ideas that would help and enrich teachers.

Conditions for Growth

Once he is moving toward a better use of process, a teacher becomes more creative and more out-going. He does, however, encounter problems, some of which may discourage him unless he can get help. There are certain conditions necessary to his continuous growth. He needs support, perspective, and refinement of skills. Let's look at these a little more closely to see how each of them may help and why it is necessary.

Support. When a new way of working seems to be ineffective and consequently the spirit of his group is poor, a teacher needs someone to help him evaluate procedures. Many times by talking the situation through with a person who understands, he can see his weaknesses for himself. When another person tells him that this is the kind of problem which many others must face regularly, he is reassured. In many school systems there is a supervisor, a principal, or a counselor who has the kind of qualities which make him trustworthy in such a capacity. Sometimes another teacher provides help and the two work together.

A teacher who is working hard to help children meet needs cooperatively operates in such a manner that he becomes more cooperative in faculty affairs, and he works so sensibly with children that other faculty members are pleased with his sincerity rather than fearful of his radical methods. He recognizes that his fellow teachers and his administrator are people of dignity and worth even though they may not share his point of view. They in turn respect him because he is a person they can trust. Peers and principal thus may add support even though they do not help him to use process more intelligently.

Perspective. In order to go beyond the superficial level in the use of the process, in order to use insight in directing experimentation, there should be a constant broadening and deepening of philosophical concepts. Talks with others, study of philosophy in general, and written analyses of experiences are a few ways of developing in this area.

Refinement of Skills. Lack of technical skills may make the work cumbersome. There should be continuous study of how learning takes place. If an individual is to progress, he needs to grow in his ability to locate and define problems. Evaluation of the group process will help refine techniques. Cooperative interaction at a high level encourages the invention of new techniques as they are needed. These should be shared with others.

The teacher should continue to study children and keep abreast of the research that will help improve his skill in working with them. He develops and refines his skills in working with parents. Relationships with people improve as he increases his skills in human relations.

New Attitudes

The use of group process brings growth in many related areas. A few of the attitudes which teachers develop follow.

A genuine interest in children. Confidence in children increases as the teacher discovers his potential as a group member. Each child is found to be a person of worth, who has a contribution to make to group thinking and action. What he has to say is worth listening to and how he feels is worth discovering. As a result of the teacher's confidence, children build confidence in themselves.

An experimental approach. The teacher develops a flexibility which makes him willing to try out different ways of working. He recognizes that experiments, no matter how carefully planned, do not always work as expected. Evaluation is important to him, and he locates and faces squarely the reasons for his failures.

Expanding interests. The number of areas in which the teacher is interested increases. He becomes increasingly well-informed, is able to see relationships, and is able to help children broaden their concepts as they plan together. Because the teacher himself is enjoying the thrill of intellectual curiosity, he stimulates children to stretch themselves intellectually.

Appreciation of nature and people. The teacher develops a deep appreciation of the so-called little things in life. The quality of relationship becomes highly important to him. Often he makes experiences for children much more meaningful because of his own depth of feeling.

Sensitivity to creative effort. The teacher is quick to recognize efforts which require creativity on the part of others. It does not matter if dozens of others have previously had similar ideas— each effort is seen as achievement for that child. Acceptance of creative efforts stimulates further efforts.

A feeling of community membership. The teacher is a person in his own right and gains the respect of friends and neighbors because he is a fine citizen. He enjoys doing things with others and his skills of cooperation show themselves not only in the school, but also in the community as a whole. His belief in people is valuable. He recognizes that he cannot solve every problem by himself and joins wholeheartedly with others. Because people feel his trust, he gains their confidence and they consider the school a part of the whole community rather than something separate. Thus, the community gains an understanding of modern education and the teacher brings to the school keen insights gained through his close association in community living.

A growing belief in himself. The teacher is growing in security as he works with others. He does not attempt to prove his own superiority by dictating to his pupils because he does not view them as potential competitors.

The teacher, in his attempt to fit himself for work in a democratic classroom, attempts to improve his own ability to work democratically. Thus as he improves his own concepts of group process, he develops the maturity which enables him to work intelligently with children.

Bibliography

Allport, Gordon W., *The Nature of Personality*. Cambridge, Mass.: Addison-Wesley Press, 1950.

Ashley-Montague, Montague Francis, *On Being Human*. New York: Henry Schuman, 1950.

Association for Supervision and Curriculum Development, *Fostering Mental Health in Our Schools*, 1950 Yearbook. Washington, D. C.: National Education Association, 1950.

Association for Supervision and Curriculum Development, *Organizing the Elementary School for Living and Learning*, 1947 Yearbook. Washington, D. C.: National Education Association, 1947.

Axline, Virginia, *Play Therapy*. New York: Houghton Mifflin, 1947.

Baruch, Dorothy W., *New Ways in Discipline*. New York: McGraw-Hill, 1949.

Benne, Kenneth and Muntyan, Bozidar, *Human Relations in Curriculum Change*. New York: Dryden Press, 1951.

Cantor, Nathaniel F., *Dynamics of Learning*. Buffalo: Foster and Stewart, 1950.

Cook, Lloyd and Forsyth, Elaine, *A Sociological Approach to Education*. New York: McGraw-Hill, 1950.

Coutu, Walter, *Emergent Human Nature. A Symbolic Field Interpretation*. New York: Knopf, 1949.

Cunningham, Ruth, *Understanding Group Behavior of Boys and Girls*. New York: Bureau of Publications, Teachers College, Columbia University, 1951.

Dewey, John, *Experience and Education*. New York: Macmillan, 1938.

Dunbar, Helen Flanders, *Mind and Body: Psychosomatic Medicine*. New York: Random House, 1947.

Elliott, Harrison S., *The Process of Group Thinking*. New York: Association Press, 1928.

Follett, Mary, *Creative Experience*. New York: Longmans, 1924.

Fromm, Erich, *Man for Himself*. New York: Rinehart, 1947.

Fromm, Erich, *Psychoanalysis and Religion*. New Haven: Yale University Press, 1950.

Giles, Harry H., *Teacher-Pupil Planning*. New York: Harper, 1941.

Hopkins, L. Thomas, "Atmosphere for Learning," *Teachers College Record*, 46:99-105.

Bibliography

Hopkins, L. Thomas, *Interaction: The Democratic Process*. Boston: D. C. Heath, 1941.

Hopkins, L. Thomas, "What Are the Essentials?" *Teachers College Record,* 46:493-500.

Horney, Karen, *Neurosis and Human Growth*. New York: Norton, 1950.

Johnson, Wendell, *People in Quandaries*. New York: Harper, 1946.

Kelley, Earl, *Education for What Is Real*. New York: Harper, 1947.

Kilpatrick, William H., *Remaking the Curriculum*. New York: Newson, 1936.

Lewin, Kurt, "Experiments on Autocratic and Democratic Atmospheres," *Social Frontiers,* 4:316-319.

Lewin, Kurt, "Field Theory of Learning," *Forty-first Yearbook,* National Society for the Study of Education, Part 2. Chicago: University of Chicago Press, 1942. Pp. 215-242.

Lynd, Robert, *Knowledge for What?* Princeton: Princeton University Press, 1939.

Miel, Alice, *Cooperative Procedures in Learning*. New York: Bureau of Publications, Teachers College, Columbia University, 1952.

Mowrer, Orval H., *Learning Theory and Personality Dynamics*. New York: Ronald Press, 1950.

Murphy, Gardner, *Personality, A Biosocial Approach to Origins and Structure*. New York: Harper, 1947.

Noar, Gertrude, *Freedom to Live and Learn*. Philadelphia: Franklin Publishing and Supply, 1948.

Olson, Willard C., *Child Development*. Boston: D. C. Heath, 1949.

Plant, James S., *The Envelope, A Study of the Impact of the World upon the Child*. New York: The Commonwealth Fund, 1937.

Plant, James S., *Personality and the Cultural Pattern*. New York: The Commonwealth Fund, 1937.

Pratt, Caroline, *I Learn from Children*. New York: Simon and Schuster, 1948.

Rasey, Marie I., *Toward Maturity*. New York: Hinds, Hayden, and Eldridge, 1947.

Redl, Fritz and Wattenberg, William, *Mental Hygiene in Teaching*. New York: Harcourt, Brace, 1941.

Roethlisberger, Fritz J., *Management and Morale*. Cambridge, Mass: Harvard University Press, 1941.

Rogers, Carl, *Client-Centered Therapy*. Boston: Houghton Mifflin, 1951.

Sharp, George, *Curriculum Development as Re-education of the Teacher*. New York: Bureau of Publications, Teachers College, Columbia University, 1951.

Slavson, Samuel R., *The Practice of Group Therapy*. New York: International Universities Press, 1947.

Snygg, Donald and Combs, Arthur W., *Individual Behavior*. New York: Harper, 1949.

Weber, Julia, *My Country School Diary*. New York: Harper, 1946.

Wiles, Kimball, *Teaching for Better Schools,* New York: Prentice Hall, 1952.

Index